PRAISE FOR *MAKING CROOKED PLACES STRAIGHT*

"What a blessing Penelope's book, *Making Crooked Places Straight*, has been to me. Her honesty in dealing with the perverse spirit in her own life encourages anyone to make the crooked straight, to overcome fears, to be free to be all he/she can be. Penelope supports the truths she discovered through a rich array of Bible verses and the meaning of those Biblical words. Her transitions from chapter to chapter allow individual journeys and hearts to be part of her act of creation, so all can have life changing encounters with the living God!"

Linaya Leaf, PhD
Retired English & Theater Professor
Former Chair of Arts & Humanities for Rocky Mountain College

"We are in a spiritual battle, and many Christians are not prepared for it. The Bible says we must not be unaware of satan's schemes, yet many of us go through life with little understanding of the invisible war all around us. Penelope Kaye's book, *Making Crooked Places Straight*, is a great tool to help open your eyes to the reality of spiritual warfare, and it provides many practical guidelines to help you overcome."

J. Lee Grady
ormer editor, *Charisma Magazine*
Director, The Mordecai Project

"Penel. ...ay s book is true manna for this age. A delightful fragrance arises throughout the pages . . . the fragrance of redemption . . . the fragrance of freedom . . . the fragrance of truth. And with this fragrance, she doesn't hide her own failings or sins. They are encompassed with humor and quickly dealt with by a well-beaten path to the door of her

Lord's heart. Because of her openness, readers are free to walk with her and receive from her vast knowledge of the perverse spirit. She exposes him, layer by layer, and strips him of his merciless disguises! Penelope created a truly unprecedented work of art with *Making Crooked Places Straight*, a tapestry laced with the Word of God, bringing strength and stability throughout the entire work."

Karen Christian
Choreographer, Liturgical Dancer, Artist

"Penelope Kaye gifts believers with an intriguing presentation of this specific, overlooked area of the dark spiritual world and what believers can do about it. I appreciate her balance of in-depth focus with broad application to many areas of Christian life and the church. Solid biblical foundations coupled with real-life experiences and practicalities make for an effective and interesting read."

Dr. Peter Lundell
Pastor, Writer, Teacher

"Penelope Kaye not only carefully articulates clearly the struggles that all of us have with perverse and invasive spirits, she lays all of her words up against the template of Scripture and bathes each topic in prayer, bringing into play the two most potent weapons of our spiritual warfare."

Michael Gantt
Author, Speaker, Missionary

Making Crooked Places Straight

MAKING Crooked PLACES STRAIGHT

*A Spiritual Warfare Journey to Become
Shining Stars in a Corrupt World*

PENELOPE KAYE

NASHVILLE

NEW YORK • LONDON • MELBOURNE • VANCOUVER

Making Crooked Places Straight

A Spiritual Warfare Journey to Become Shining Stars in a Corrupt World

Published in New York, New York, by Morgan James Publishing. Morgan James is a trademark of Morgan James, LLC. www.MorganJamesPublishing.com

ISBN 9781642791938 paperback
ISBN 9781642791945 eBook
Library of Congress Control Number: 2018908257

Cover Design by:
Lori Bonifay
Voice of Hope Creative Designs

Interior Design by:
Chris Treccani
www.3dogcreative.net

Illustrations by:
Haley Hoffner

Morgan James is a proud partner of Habitat for Humanity Peninsula and Greater Williamsburg. Partners in building since 2006.

Get involved today! Visit
MorganJamesPublishing.com/giving-back

In
Honor
of
Ilah Glee Stevens
1936-2009

Ilah carried this book in her spirit years

before I wrote one word.

Without her encouragement, love, and prayers,

Making Crooked Places Straight would still be in the closet.

CONTENTS

INTRODUCTION

I pondered much about writing this introduction, whether it was even necessary. I originally wrote my own foreword before discovering authors don't do that particular task. Not until finishing round five of editing, did I realize it didn't even qualify as a foreword, but was, in fact, the synopsis. The intro almost ended in the cyberspace trash bin until God dropped two thoughts into my heart—the story behind the contract and the story behind the beginning of each chapter.

First, the contract tale. My writing passion is picture books. Creating stories for children to help their spirits grow and make them laugh, often at the same time, causes my heart to sing. At past writers conferences, this focus directed me to industry people connected to children's publishing. During my second Colorado Christian Writers Conference, I zeroed in on those open to picture books. This led me to Terry Whalin, acquisitions editor for Morgan James Publishing. We spent most of my one-on-one meeting discussing my various manuscripts. At the very, very last minute, I mentioned my spiritual warfare project including the following:

- This is a necessary book for the times we live in.
- Christians need to understand how the perverse spirit works.
- People will buy the book.

Terry looked at me and said, "I think I want you to send me your book."

A bit astonished, I double-checked with him. Until this moment, the manuscript lived in my closet because I didn't think anyone wanted to read a book about a perverse spirit, let alone publish one. He assured me that he wanted to see it. I said OK.

When I arrived home, he sent an email, reminding me to send it. Still hesitant, I called him in late May, a couple weeks after the conference. I told him it needed editing, especially after learning more about the craft of writing in Colorado. He said not to worry; he had read hundreds of manuscripts in various stages of editing. Still doubtful, I agreed to send it when I felt ready.

For the next six weeks, my routine consisted of coming home from my day job, grabbing a bite to eat, and working on my manuscript. One emphasis centered on eliminating "that," apparently one of my favorite words. A search revealed I liked it 778 times! Armed with more editing tips, I ruthlessly attacked the pages. By mid-July, approximately 30 pages and 7,000 words, including 576 uses of "that," found a home in the trash bin.

And then, doubts plagued me. Should I or shouldn't I? Did I dare risk putting my pain in the hands of strangers, regardless of their benefits? The answer eluded me. Calendar pages landed in the garbage three times while the manuscript languished in the confines of my computer. Misgivings continued to assail me.

One October night, I engaged in a staring competition with the monitor. The winner? Not me. In an email to Terry, I apologized for the delay, shared my reservations, attached the manuscript, and hit Send. I walked away with no expectation of hearing back. Besides, piles of laundry and a sink full of dishes clamored for attention. Several hours later, I prepared for bed. Reaching to turn off the computer for the night, his bolded name kept my finger in mid-air. My first thought? *Well, this is different.* My second thought? *Wait 'til he reads it. I won't hear back.*

Two weeks later my cell phone vibrated at work. Terry was on the other end. He told me he liked the manuscript. Surprised to hear his voice and comments, I thanked him. He proceeded to tell me the next step, which was to send it to a pastor on staff to make sure the book held sound theological doctrine, no heresies, no crazy, off-the-wall teachings. I said OK. Again. Then he mentioned the pastor's denomination—Baptist. Red flags, warning bells, screaming sirens all went off inside my head. From my perspective, Baptists didn't like, approve, or believe in the spiritual warfare I covered in my book. Terry tried to reassure me, and we continued our discussion about the book and Morgan James. Still, in my mind, this deal had blown up like the grand finale of the annual 4th of July fireworks display in my hometown. I spent the next weeks focusing on my children's books.

The day before Thanksgiving, my phone vibrated on my desk. Again. I said hello and heard Terry's voice on the other end. He wanted to be the first to congratulate me. Morgan James wanted to publish my book! Speechless for the first several minutes, a real conversation eventually occurred. At one point, I asked how it happened. He told me the Baptist pastor liked my book and went to bat for me at the publishing board meeting, resulting in a yes from the committee. Complete befuddlement took over my mind as I realized God and the Baptist pastor had blown up my neat little prejudices about this denomination beyond fireworks. Even the eruption of Mount Vesuvius paled in comparison.

After we finished our call, I sat at my desk, humbled and grateful beyond words. Never did I imagine signing a contract for this book. Yet, multiple answered prayers took place over the next several months, all culminating with you holding *Making Crooked Places Straight* in your hands. A miracle from God's hands!

Now, the tale of the chapter beginnings. Years ago, with the writing project in its early stages, Chapter One unfolded in a matter of days. Looking forward to Chapter Two, I sat in front of my computer and . . . zilch. I took a break, came back, and . . . zero. Throughout the day . . . nothing. The next morning white space appeared to mock me, daring me to type something. This continued for days, then weeks. The transition from the end of Chapter One to the start of Chapter Two managed to escape my thought processes. After six long weeks, I finally reached out to Ilah, my dear friend. As she prayed, God showed her a picture:

I am swimming in a river, moving downstream with the current. I avoid various obstacles, including boulders, logjams, and rapids. At some point, I get out of the river and walk uphill.

Ilah sensed the Lord wanted me to go back upstream to the beginning of the river to find my answer. After we hung up, confusion still swirled in my mind. The river obviously represented my writing journey, but what did God mean by going back upstream? To the beginning of what? The blank page stared at me for several more days.

Finally, the answer plopped into my imagination like a raindrop falling on a lake, fanning ripples across the water. Grinning, I plopped into my chair and went back to the beginning of Chapter One. The words tumbled onto the page in near desperate fashion. On the first page of Chapter Two, they almost fell into the empty space. Each transition slid with the ease of otters zipping down a riverbank, splashing in the water.

What brought such joy? A character who questions, argues, and doubts the premises of the titles in the early chapters. As the book moves forward, this person's demeanor slowly and painfully shifts. Until . . . well, that would be a bit of a spoiler so I'll stop. Feel free to ponder the motives of this unnamed individual. Who knows? They might match some of your own.

Although the introduction ends here, hopefully, the journey ahead leads to wild, crazy, life-changing encounters with the Living God. Thank you for letting me share in your life through *Making Crooked Places Straight*.

Blessings,

Penelope Kaye

PS: Some info regarding formatting:

- All italics, bold type, and extra parentheses/brackets within Scriptures are my emphasis, not the original text, unless the reference is the Amplified Bible.

- An asterisk * next to a name denotes all names within that particular section have been changed.
- The footnotes for Strong's Concordance have numbers in plain text and italics. The plain text denotes definitions from the Hebrew dictionary for Old Testament words, and the italics text denotes definitions from the Greek dictionary for New Testament words. This follows Strong's pattern, which allows readers to find the correct definition. Also, for those who like to delve into word studies, you will notice footnotes with more than one number. I used commas to separate those following the progression back to the original root words; I used semi-colons to separate numbers with individual root meanings.
- Throughout the book, I have written about Holy Spirit, deliberately not using "the" in front of "Holy." This is on purpose. A few years back, a number of national spiritual leaders pointed out that no one puts "the" in front of a person's name, such as "the Paul" or "the Matthew." Yet, in our conversations, we have referred to the Third Person of the Trinity as "the Holy Spirit." As a result, a concerted effort by many of these leaders led to dropping "the" before Holy Spirit. Although it was hard to remember at first, I too chose to leave off "the" when referring to Him. Now it seems odd to say His name any differently.

CHAPTER 1

The Beginning

A perverse spirit? Who, me? In my church? How could you even think such a thing? Why, our church has the best worship this side of heaven! Our pastor preaches sermons so uplifting you would think God was standing in the pulpit. And as for me, I help in the church. I give over and above the tithe. I support other ministries, including two children in third-world countries. I read the Bible and pray, and not just before meals. I'm certainly not perfect, but a perverse spirit? Surely you jest! Of course, I know it's in the world. Why, the homosexual agenda is running rampant all over the place. Just take a look at what's on television, not to mention the big screen! And have you listened to some of the music out there? Talk about perverse! But not me, not my church. A perverse spirit? No way!

Yes, you. Yes, in your church. Shocking? Yes. Appalling? Yes. Deplorable? Yes, all that and more. The most insidious of evil spirits, the perverse spirit lays claim as the "granddaddy" of them all. How is this possible? To discover the answer, we need to go back to the days of perfection in heaven. Days of matchless beauty, awesome majesty, perfect . . . until the day . . . What day? The day sin found a place in heaven, through Lucifer.

However, before we start our journey to discover and uncover the characteristics marking the perverse spirit, let's pray:

Father God, you are the Maker of heaven and earth. We praise and glorify you. Thank you for leading us into your truth concerning the perverse spirit. We humble ourselves before you. Cover us with the precious blood of Jesus. Open our eyes to see and recognize perverseness in our own thoughts and actions. Give us the desire and the grace to press on to wholeness, in spirit, soul, and body. Only you, Almighty God, can make the crooked places straight so we can shine like stars. We bless you, in Jesus' name. Amen.

Since we're on this journey together, I probably need to share how I came to write about the perverse spirit. I never intended to do a study on this crooked serpent, let alone write a book. I far prefer to worship God, dance before Him, and share sweet communion with Him. But He had a different idea; He just had to bring me to the place where I was willing.

Because God created us, He knows what makes us tick, what makes our hearts sing. For me, it's word studies. Although I'm not a biblical scholar, I love to look up words in Strong's Concordance.[1] I enjoy discovering what they mean and how to apply them to my life.

One morning years ago, while praying for my deeply dysfunctional marriage, I felt impressed by the Lord to read Psalm 101:

I will sing of mercy and justice;
To You, O Lord, I will sing praises.
I will behave wisely in a perfect way.
Oh, when will you come to me?
I will walk within my house with a perfect heart.
I will set nothing wicked before my eyes;
I hate the work of those who fall away;

It shall not cling to me.

A *perverse* heart shall depart from me;

I will not know wickedness. (vv. 1–4)

Contemplating these verses, I realized God wanted me to recognize that a perverse spirit was the culprit behind the trouble. With the added stress of my own life issues and caring for a baby, this revelation went on the proverbial back burner. The following year my marriage came under greater attack. I remembered Psalm 101 and the perverse spirit. My thought at the time? *Maybe I should look this up so I know what I'm up against.* Oh, the bliss of ignorance!

What I discovered completely altered my life. I found myself in a whirlpool, which was sucking the life out of me. Throughout the days, then weeks that I worked on the study, my friend, Teresa remained loyal, always encouraging me to stay the course and not quit. After nearly two months of intense spiritual warfare, and only a little of the initial work left, I finally called Teresa and Brenda, another friend, for prayer before starting on the study. Consequently, a great deal of the warfare lifted.

When I finished it, I wanted to share my discoveries. Completely naïve, I assumed others would be excited to learn about my work. The results over the next several months? Raw, brutal, and gut-wrenching changes. My husband, who had left me shortly before I started the study, checked into a mental hospital. Eventually, my marriage ended in divorce. I became a single mom with a toddler and an infant, something I promised myself would never happen. Because some relatives believed me to be a religious fanatic, the ever-widening family chasm led to more estrangement. Some Christians believed I had let go of my faith and stepped into rebellion. Friends stopped fellowshipping with me. I remember times of agonizing sobs, wondering if I would ever be whole.

One night I had a horrible nightmare:

I am in my living room with Jesus. He leaves me for another beautiful woman. In the next scene, I am looking out the kitchen window. On the balcony of the four-plex next door, a gorilla-type demon screams like a banshee. Intending to get help, I open the front door. There stands the monster, screaming in my face. I shut the door. I'm immediately back in the kitchen, looking out the window, seeing the screaming demon. I go back to the door, open it, and see the demon screaming at me again. The cycle continues throughout the dream.

I woke up terrified, fully expecting to see the demon standing at the foot of my bed. I felt alone and abandoned, overwhelmed with the knowledge of this perverse spirit that appeared to have me in a vice grip, determined to keep me in bondage.

Meeting so much opposition and spiritual warfare, I put the study in a file, put the file in the filing cabinet, closed the door, and kept my mouth shut. How long? Eighteen years. Few people knew anything about it. If someone asked for prayer, and I sensed a perverse spirit lurking around, I prayed silently. Only when backed into a corner did I mention the possibility of this particular demonic entity, and only if I thought the person could handle hearing it.

However, Ilah, a woman I met three years after finishing it, did press me about my notes. She asked about them on a regular basis and insisted on getting a copy. I finally relented. We met for a quick lunch, and I handed over the infamous study. In between peanut butter and homemade peach jelly sandwiches, I explained the process I used throughout the research, including the chicken scratch page.[2] After describing the spiritual warfare I endured, I cautioned, "Please don't share it with just anybody."

She listened intently, jotting down her own chicken scratches.

A couple of hours later, I headed home. And from that moment on, the perverse spirit study set up a permanent home in my filing cabinet behind a closed door.

Ilah, meanwhile, had other ideas. She called a few days later and, after a bit of chit-chat, got to the purpose for contacting me.

"I've been praying with a friend for quite a while, and we're not making much progress. I really think the perverse spirit is behind it."

"That would not surprise me."

"Well, what do you think of my sending her a copy of your notes?"

Deeply opposed to having those pages in someone else's hands, intense discussions followed. In the end, Ilah prevailed. The study went out. I reminded her not to send the "chicken scratch" page, and she agreed; but somehow it went out as well. This happened several times. Each time I resisted, yet Ilah discerned God's leading. Was it? Probably. My concern stemmed from all the warfare I went through putting the study together. I didn't want anyone else to undergo the same spiritual attacks nor did I want any more backlash. Yet, God held me together in spite of my fears.

After a few years, our paths went different directions, and I seldom saw Ilah. We did meet for dinner once when my daughters and I traveled through her city on our way home from a conference. As the four of us chatted, she asked me, "Have you done anything yet about getting the perverse spirit study in a book?"

I had expected her question. Ilah always wanted it to be in print because, in her mind, she literally believed it would help multitudes of people.

"No," I said, having no desire to pull *that* file out of *that* drawer, even though more than a decade had passed since the initial work.

"I really believe this is a necessary book, Penelope. I keep seeing images of people standing in line for it. Please pray about it."

"OK," I agreed and promptly ignored the request. My computer mouse suddenly contracted the plague.

More years went by. Then the phone rang one morning. I picked it up and heard Ilah's voice.

"Hello! Can you believe it's me?"

"Ilah, what a wonderful surprise! What's going on?"

"Well, I somehow misplaced my copy of the perverse spirit study. I've looked everywhere and simply can't find it. Would you mind sending me another copy? And by the way, have you thought any more about putting it in a book?"

I paused before answering. Only a couple of weeks before, I thought of opening *that* drawer and taking out *that* file. As much as I wanted to, I couldn't lie. I took a deep breath and told her the truth.

"You know, it's been in the closet all these years, but two weeks ago, I suddenly thought of getting it out again."

"That's wonderful! I'm so glad. Keep me in the loop. And in the meantime, I'll be praying."

After we hung up, I stood in the kitchen staring at the closet. I knew opening the door would change my life forever. I began to pray—seriously. Sensing a strong leading from God to actually write the book, I checked with three friends who knew of the study. They all responded with "Praise God!" I didn't go that far. Still, the path ahead beckoned while memories taunted.

Feeling helpless to resist, I eventually opened *that* drawer and pulled out *that* file. As I pondered and prayed, the phone rang again. It was my new friend, Heidi, who knew nothing about the perverse spirit because I never talked about it. I shared Ilah's call with her and a little from my notes. After listening for several minutes, she said, "You've got to do this book! I need it! Other people need it! It's our life!"

If that wasn't enough confirmation, God gave me a dream:

I am in a classroom writing about the perverse spirit. The room turns into a church. I try to write about other things. Those words disappear. I see myself writing about the perverse spirit again. As I do, images from my past keep popping up, particularly those of my ex-husband.

Obviously, I wanted to write about other things. God definitely wanted me to write about the perverse spirit, not only in the world, but especially in the church. It was also clear I had to deal with past wounds still affecting my future. Nothing about it gave me Holy Ghost goose bumps. Still, I knew what I needed to do.

The next day, Friday, I wrote the first page. I shared it with a couple of friends, and they liked what they heard. On Monday, I became sick with what I knew were symptoms brought on by the perverse spirit. This lasted two days.

On Wednesday, my daughters came home from gymnastics bruised and in pain. Their teammates forgot to spot them or catch them. Consequently, someone kicked them in the face or they landed on their faces more than once. After dinner, Rebekah, my youngest, received an obscene text message.

On Thursday, a woman rear-ended my car. I knew full well what was happening, and I called friends for prayer. I also quit writing. The attacks stopped. The book sat in cyberspace for over a month. An easy out? The power cord to my computer went on the fritz. I conveniently didn't call to replace it for several weeks.

The new year began. I still hesitated to write about the perverse spirit. Yet, I felt compelled by Holy Spirit to press forward. I called Heidi, and the two of us met almost daily for two weeks. We broke generational curses dealing with the blessing from a father. We worked through word curses from sources too numerous to list. These covered the work of my hands, the creativity God placed in my hands, my view of work for the sake of work, the lies of never being good enough. A beloved father figure had spoken over me, "No one wants to listen to you!" That lie added to others regarding the value of my words.

From there, we dealt with my view of always being someone's "whore" and only valued because of the work someone could get out of me, including God. These curses kept the gift of writing in a state of impotency. I had all the necessary equipment, but no power or drive to bring to fulfillment what God ordained for me. We laid the axe to the root of each one. I renounced, repented, forgave, and blessed. Heidi anointed and blessed my hands again and again. We spoke God's Word, His truth, over them. The day arrived when I embraced not only the gift of writing, I embraced the writer God created me to be—Penelope Kaye.

In the midst of this healing and deliverance, God gave me a dream showing His unfathomable love:

I am at my parents' home in the back yard. It seems to be a large gathering of sorts, and I'm supposed to meet someone. Everything seems wispy in the dream. I can't make out individual people. In the next scene, I'm back in my house, which is a cluttered mess. Heaps of clothes dominate the living room: Clean clothes. Dirty clothes. Clothes to be folded. Clothes to be ironed. Clothes hanging up in every conceivable place, along with a few inconceivable spots. Dishes fill both sinks. Piles of books and papers cover tables, countertops, and chairs. A total disaster! The doorbell rings. I open the door and shout, "Grace! You're here!" I throw my arms around Grace, who hugs me back. With a big smile, Grace walks into the living room in the middle of my calamity and sits down.

Pondering the dream, I realized God's Spirit of Grace waited at the door of my heart, and my messy life didn't matter. Grace came in smiling, happy to be in the midst of my catastrophe. The most amazing aspect of the dream? Grace arrived in the form of a man. This seemed rather odd until I remembered 2 Corinthians 12:9, "My grace is sufficient for you . . ."

Our American understanding of "sufficient" is enough to get by, which could not be farther from the truth. Studying the term, I discovered it carries the idea of *raising a barrier to ward off the enemy.*[3] What a powerful revelation! That's why God sent Grace to my house in the form of a man. While a lovely name for girls, we have assumed God's grace retains feminine qualities. However, ribbons and lace do not come to mind in the midst of a battle. I needed absolute assurance of God's protection while exposing the perverse spirit. God's grace would be, and has been, an undeniably potent weapon in bringing this revelation to print.

On a personal level, I believe God had another reason for presenting Grace as a man and not a woman. For nearly twenty years, I raised my daughters with no man in the picture. In all honesty, I didn't need another woman in our house—I needed a man. And this man? My, my, my! He was the best-looking male specimen I had ever laid eyes on! His gorgeous thick, black hair curled a bit. Piercing, deep blue eyes sparkled. His brilliant smile dulled the sun. A pair of dimples added the finishing touch. And not the least bit put off by the mess. Grace plopped down on the couch, delighted to be in my home. The chaos in my life did not deter him. Because of the difficult and messy path ahead, I needed not only God's grace for protection, but also His joy for strength.

Sharing the dream with my intercessors, I laughed and cried at the goodness of God. Since then, I have started paraphrasing Romans 5:8, saying, "While we are in our messes, God sends Grace to us." Thank God, thank God, thank God for His grace.

At this juncture, one would have thought I was ready to write. That person would be wrong. I had an idea why but didn't want to admit it. A week after the dream, another friend, Lisha, came over. We chatted a bit, and then prayed quietly for a few minutes. Suddenly, laughter bubbled out of her. In the midst of chuckles, she said, "God just showed me a picture of a minuscule you climbing out of a gigantic inkwell, dripping with ink, completely exasperated. A massive Jesus sat across from the inkwell gazing at you with total love, joy, and adoration."

Lisha turned to look at me, and more laughter ensued. "You have the exact expression on your face that you had in my vision."

I glared at her, and finally, in frustration, let the truth spill out.

"Look, I don't want to write about the perverse spirit. It's ugly, it's cruel, it's wicked! Besides, I lost too much just doing the study. I'm not this naïve little Christian anymore to think the devil's going to let this get written without me paying a price. No thanks."

I closed my eyes and pursed my lips, shaking my head as memories flashed in my mind. I expected intense, even debilitating, warfare to get this book into print. I had counted the cost. I had too much at stake to risk opening *that* drawer again.

"But, Pen," Lisha said, using her pet nickname for me, "without writing the book, no one will know about the perverse spirit. If you expose him, you bring freedom to me, to everyone who will read it. And God will give you the desires of your heart."

"Lisha, I'm afraid. You don't know how awful it was. I can't do it again. I can't."

"Oh, Pen, God's got this. He trusts you to do this. You need to trust Him."

As the realization of Lisha's words penetrated my fears—God did indeed trust me—I also understood that He had equipped me and would protect me as I put words on paper, or more specifically, in a word document.

This time I closed my eyes and, with tears in my voice, whispered, "Yes." God had given me His promise. One way or another, *Making Crooked Places Straight* would find its way into the hands of those desperately seeking freedom from the bondages of this vile, evil, vicious perverse spirit. A number of trusted intercessors covered me in prayer during the time I dipped my pen in heaven's inkwell and put words on paper. I want the same for you. As we begin, join me before the throne of grace in prayer:

Father God, only you know how desperate our hearts cry out to be free. Only you know how to make our crooked places straight. Thank you for grace, your infinite, wonderful, marvelous grace. When overwhelming darkness smothers us, your grace renews our strength. When obstacles cause us to stumble and fall, your grace lifts us up. When life comes crushing down on us, your grace leads us to still waters where we find our rest in you. We trust you and praise you, in Jesus' name. Amen.

Are you ready? The pages await us.

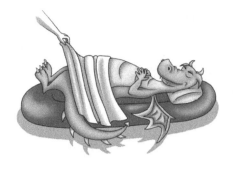

CHAPTER 2

Uncovering the Dragon

OK, I have to admit I'm a little curious. You said Psalm 101 mentions the perverse spirit. And you did a study about it so it must be in other verses too. I don't get it. If this is in the Bible, why have I never seen it before? Why hasn't anyone preached on it except to talk about homosexuals? I mean, that's what the perverse spirit is all about, homosexuality, right? I know I don't have to be concerned. But, I guess I am a little curious.

"Curiosity killed the cat," the old saying goes. However, in my case, curiosity uncovered the perverse spirit. Because of my love for word studies, when I read the Bible and come across something puzzling, I check out Strong's Concordance and Webster's dictionary. Invariably, God gives me insight and revelation to exhort, instruct, convict, or prove the truth of the Word of God. Paul's second letter to his spiritual son still holds true today (2 Timothy 4:2).

Since Bible apps didn't exist the day I decided to look into the perverse spirit, I grabbed Strong's. And my, my, my! What a Pandora's box I opened! At least it looked like Pandora's box. In reality, I unlocked a treasure chest.

My mouth dropped open again and again. I was walking out Isaiah 45:2–3 and didn't even know it:

> I will go before you and make the *crooked* places straight; I will break in pieces the gates of bronze and cut the bars of iron. I will give you the treasures of darkness and hidden riches of secret places, that you may know that I, the LORD, who call you by your name, am the God of Israel.

God, in His wisdom and endless love, pledged beforehand to make those crooked places straight. He promised treasures and riches hidden for lifetimes. Even now, as I write these words, I'm amazed He chose me to do this work, someone profoundly bound up by a wicked spirit. Yet, isn't it just like our glorious Lord? Take a minute to pray and praise with me:

Oh God, words seem completely inadequate when we praise you. If I spoke this prayer instead of writing it, I would break out in tongues. You are the Great I AM, the Alpha and Omega! Hallelujah to the King of kings! Nothing is impossible with you. Your promises are Yes and Amen, always. Thank you for making our crooked places straight, for breaking the bondages holding us captive, for giving us treasures of wisdom and understanding, for setting us free to shine like stars. You are so worthy, so holy, Lord God Almighty, in Jesus' name. Amen.

Treasures of Darkness?

Wow! Treasures of darkness? Hidden riches? Although I didn't think anything good could possibly come from such an ugly, repulsive word, I found a gold mine of revelation—the beginning of crooked places becoming straight. What exactly did I uncover? For starters, the Old and New Testament writers used a form of *perverse* fifty-one times with nineteen different root words. Even more surprising, only two showed a connection to moral deficiency. Only two. One-tenth. Put another way, nine-tenths of the root meanings for *perverse* have nothing to do with sexual immorality. I expected it to be the opposite. Instead, 90 percent of the meanings for *perverse* have nothing to do with deviant sexual behavior. Does that shock  you as much as it did me? I'm going to repeat it—90 percent of the root meanings for *perverse* have nothing to do with perverted sex.

For decades we, the church, assumed *perverse* only related to homosexuals and sexual perversions. Looking at it with the light of God's truth, we find other revealing meanings. For instance, one original root means *to be rash and hurl headlong*;[4] another denotes *worry and weary*;[5] still another definition is *to be meddlesome*.[6] No sexual deviant behavior there; yet, that's exactly where our laser-beam focus went. Even more humbling? Seeing the perverse spirit at work in me. Embarrassing. Humiliating. Appalling. I felt exposed. I feared everyone else could see it in me and think the worst. Many times I wanted to give up. But with a desperation born out of a desire for freedom, I pressed on and pressed into God. I had no other hope.

Are you ready to take the plunge? If you're honest, you may want to run as far and fast as you can. Don't. Anchor your soul in the promise from heaven and in Jesus, the Living Word. Rest your hope in this truth from Numbers 23:19, "God is not a man, that He should lie, nor a son of man, that He should repent. Has He said, and will He not do? Or has He spoken, and will He not make it good?" God will make the crooked places straight in your life and mine. It's a Yes and Amen promise!

Need a Wrench?

To begin, look in Exodus 23:8, the first time a form of *perverse* is used in Scripture, "And you shall take no bribe, for a bribe blinds the discerning and *perverts* the words of the righteous." The primary root here means *to wrench or overthrow*.[7] Jehovah God warned the Israelites that bribes cause words to be wrenched and overthrown.

How about bringing this meaning a little closer to home? Have you ever had something *wrenched* from you? I'm not referring to an actual object in your hand, but something in the unseen realm forcefully taken from you. Perhaps a dream, a promise, a vision? Mine? The day I knew my marriage ended. I felt like someone took a knife and cut my womb open. Every dream, vision, prophecy, everything I held onto for my marriage vanished. Excruciating pain ripped 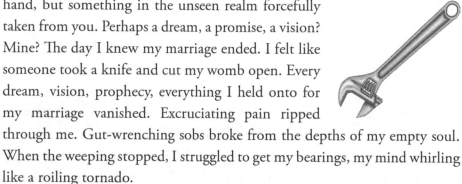 through me. Gut-wrenching sobs broke from the depths of my empty soul. When the weeping stopped, I struggled to get my bearings, my mind whirling like a roiling tornado.

Clearly, I don't know the specifics of your situation. Maybe a marriage, maybe a ministry, maybe something else. Whatever wreckage you experienced, a perverse spirit whipped the winds of destruction. I have a sense this revelation stirred up trauma in some of you. Whether from a fresh wound or a buried one, let's take a few minutes to pray:

Father God, only you know the depths of our devastation, the promises ripped from us, and the raw pain left behind. Let your healing balm flow over us, going into the darkest depths of our beings. When a memory surfaces, and the pain overwhelms again, let your gentle touch remind us we are not alone; we are not abandoned. We have a Father who knows our name and comforts us. Thank you, Lord, in Jesus' name. Amen.

At this juncture, you may want to put the book down and never pick it up again. Please don't. Please know that I understand your agony. I've spent several hours sobbing, trying to pick up the pen again and again, only to weep more. Believe me when I say God is bigger—bigger than the wrench used against you, bigger than the pain wrenching your insides, bigger than this monster.

When I wrote Chapter One, I have to be honest and tell you I had no faith I would ever be free from the perverse spirit. As a matter of fact, I didn't think anyone could be free. I was only writing out of obedience to God. Somewhere in the first lines of Chapter Two, the faith of God began to fill me with joy and delight. I knew, I really knew, I would be healed, delivered, and free of this hideous viper; and not just me, but everyone else as well. So even if you don't think you'll be healed, I do. Even if you can't see your deliverance, I can. Even if you don't believe you'll be free, I do. Even if you don't have any faith, God has given me enough faith to believe for you. As you press on with me and discover these treasures of darkness and hidden riches, the light of God's truth will set you free, and you will be free indeed. I won't let go of you; I promise. Neither will God. He's on your side. Don't ever let go of that truth, no matter what it looks like. God is on your side. Always. Forever.

As you meditate on Him and His truth, I want to share an incident that happened during my study. Only a few weeks into the research, I came across this particular meaning of *wrench*. Rather startled, I called Teresa to tell her what I found. We chatted briefly and hung up. Less than ten minutes later, the phone rang.

"You're not going to believe what just happened!" I heard Teresa's breathless voice on the other end. Ministering to the downtrodden, she lived in a low-income area notorious for alcoholics, drug addicts, and prostitutes. Over the years, I had heard many tales of the antics and exploits that took place in her neighborhood.

"What's going on now?"

"After we hung up, one of the well-known prostitutes around here burst into our house waving a wrench!"

"What? You're kidding?"

"No! She didn't even knock, just yanked the door open. She ran through the living room, into the kitchen, and out the back door, whirling this wrench, screaming like a wild banshee."

"You're serious?"

"Absolutely. I'm completely astonished."

"Did any of you get hurt?"

"No, it happened too fast. We all just froze, our mouths hanging open. All I can say, sister, is you are on the right track. Keep on digging."

After saying goodbye, I stood in the kitchen, my thoughts racing. Without a doubt, the enemy felt threatened, and he didn't like it one bit. The once simple Bible study took a sudden lurch to unknown depths. My discernment levels went up several notches; still, I determined to persevere. Had I known how long it would take to complete the study or the price I would pay to cross the finish line . . . ? ? ? Question marks seem appropriate because I don't have an answer. However, I cringe at the thought of what my life would be today had I stopped. And you certainly would not be reading *Making Crooked Places Straight*. Thank God for His faithfulness!

Which Government Was Overthrown?

On a larger scale, look at the other meaning in this root word: *Overthrow*.[8] In the 1900s alone, more than three hundred attempted coup d'états took place across the globe, some succeeding and others failing.[9] I don't intend to start a political discussion nor am I saying, "Thus saith the Lord." However, I do want to suggest that if Holy Spirit did not lead and direct godly men and women to pray, fast, and seek the Lord for His plans and purposes for their nation, a perverse spirit probably worked behind the scenes in the governmental change.

In bringing this meaning to a more personal level, we expose another similar treasure of darkness to the light of truth: *Turned upside down*.[10] Has your world ever turned upside down without you knowing how it happened? And I'm not talking about the time the apostles were accused of turning the world upside down for preaching Jesus (Acts 17:6). I'm referring to a time your entire world turned upside down because a perverse spirit had free rein. I will never forget the day I had my "six-month" evaluation ten months after I started my position at a local company.

Beginning with positive statements, my supervisor soon changed to lies and baseless accusations from supposed complaints about my performance. The long and short of it—fired. Completely illegal, unethical, immoral. My world turned upside down. I felt devastated, for me, my family, and the unfinished assignment God spoke into my heart—to pray my coworkers into the kingdom and the company into the end-time harvest. Instead, a perverse spirit turned loose had thrown a wrench into the heart of God's plans.

Perhaps this describes your life, and you have had no respite from the agony engulfing your days and nights. Let me carry you to the throne of grace in prayer:

Lord God, I bring your precious lambs to you. Broken and hurt, frightened and weary, they need the comfort of our Good Shepherd. Soothe their troubled souls as only you can. Keep them in the bosom of your heart. Whisper hope-filled words into their deepest pain. Carry them through the darkest of nights until they step into the light of your dear Son, in Jesus' name. Amen.

Agonizing as this time may be, press into God and trust Him. Somehow, some day, He will bring you into a broad place with pleasant lines, just like He promised David in Psalm 18.

Words Turned Every Which Way But Loose!

More nuggets and hidden treasures await us. I discovered several interchangeable King James Version terms coming from the same Hebrew roots as *perverse*: *Froward* (I honestly thought it was another word for forward—wrong);[11] *untoward* (I thought it was the opposite of toward—wrong);[12] *iniquity* (I didn't discover this one until a couple of years after the initial study—I knew it had to do with sin, but had no clue how it related to *perverse*);[13] and *crooked* (I actually saw the connection—the only one that made sense).[14] Look at a sampling of Scriptures, all from the King James Version:

. . . the man that speaketh *froward* things; who leave[s] the paths of uprightness, to walk in the ways of darkness; who rejoice[s] to do evil, and delight[s] in the *frowardness* of the wicked; whose ways are *crooked*, and . . . *froward* in [his] paths . . . (Prov. 2:12b–15)

. . . but the *froward* tongue shall be cut out. (Prov. 10:31)

. . . but the mouth of the wicked speaketh *frowardness*. (Prov. 10:32)

. . . and the mouth of the wicked devoureth *iniquity*. (Prov. 19:28)

. . . The words of his mouth are *iniquity* and deceit: he hath left off to be wise, and to do good. (Ps. 36:3)

And with many other words did [Peter] testify and exhort, saying, Save yourselves from this *untoward* generation. (Acts 2:40)

The shared meaning in all these verses has to do with *turn, i.e., overthrow, overturn, turn about or over, turn to the contrary, turn every way*.[15] We find it in Proverbs 17:20 where " . . . he who has a *perverse* tongue falls into evil" and Jeremiah 23:36 where man has ". . . *perverted* the words of the living God . . ." Throughout the study, words and the perverse spirit connected repeatedly.

If you think back to past discussions, you can probably pinpoint the moment the conversation turned. Perhaps, in the midst of a confrontation, others turned your words every which way but the truth. Or you unwittingly found yourself in a heated argument that had nothing to do with the original conversation. Maybe the one listening heard something totally different than what you said. I am not talking about differences between men and women, personality types, simple misunderstandings, or someone just not paying attention. I'm referring to the cunning moves of a perverse spirit.

I cannot begin to recount the number of times in my marriage that demon twisted and turned our words every which way but the right way. I remember one incident when Holly, my oldest, was about fifteen months old. My husband had disciplined her out of anger and frustration. When the dust finally settled and she fell asleep, we attempted to discuss it. No matter how

I suggested he could have done things differently, he kept repeating, "I was wrong, but I handled it right. I was wrong, but I handled it right." A clear sign of a perverse spirit slithering in our family once again.

Another incident happened with my youngest daughter, Rebekah, when she was about six. Celebrating 4th of July at my parents' home, Rebekah and my brother-in-law were in the midst of a conversation. My sister and I stood about two feet away. We overheard Rebekah speak in a very disrespectful tone. We both scolded her, and I insisted she apologize. She looked shocked and hurt, but still obeyed me. My brother-in-law, on the other hand, looked at the two of us as if we had suddenly grown three ears in the middle of our foreheads. He defended Rebekah and flat out denied she said anything out of line. My sister and I insisted; he didn't back down. I finally asked her what she had said. Taken aback to find out it was an innocent question, my sister and I both apologized. I scooped her up, loved on her, and asked her to forgive me, which she did.

To emphasize the maneuvers of this wily serpent, in the two hundredths of a second it took for us to hear Rebekah's words, a perverse spirit turned them to the contrary. The result? A serious reprimand for my daughter. Had I not humbled myself to restore a right relationship with her, the perverse spirit would have done his job in sowing discord in my family. Scriptures describe this cunning attribute:

Frowardness is in his heart, he deviseth mischief continually; he soweth discord. (Prov. 6:14 KJV)

A *froward* man soweth strife . . . (Prov. 16:28 KJV)

Although these verses use *froward*, they share the same meaning of *perverse* with all of its intended results. As we continue to uncover more of the characteristics of this demonic entity, you will be stunned over and over at the ease with which this evil viper wreaks havoc and destruction through the spoken word.

Cruel and Unusual Words of Punishment

I want to discuss one more hidden nugget regarding words: *Viciousness*.[16] Cruel and vicious words pierce the souls and spirits of many, leading to warped views of themselves and others, including God. The King James Version in Proverbs 15:4 paints an accurate description, "A wholesome tongue is a tree of life: but *perverseness* therein is a breach in the spirit."

To fully understand the depth of damage this particular perverseness causes, we need to dig a little deeper for our treasure. *Breach* comes from a Hebrew word with the idea of *fracture*.[17] Other meanings include *bruise, destruction, and hurt*. When vicious words pierce like daggers, you can rest assured a perverse spirit will ravage the life of its intended victim.

Even Scripture refers to words as weapons again and again. One passage, Psalm 64:2b–3, describes the deadly force of words, ". . . workers of *iniquity*, who sharpen their tongue[s] like a sword, and bend their bows to shoot their arrows—bitter words."

In the New Testament, James wrote his own graphic description of an untamed tongue in chapter 3, verses 6, 8, "And the tongue is a fire, a world of *iniquity*. The tongue is so set among our members that it defiles the whole body, and sets on fire the course of nature; and it is set on fire by hell . . . But no man can tame the tongue. It is an unruly evil, full of deadly poison." As a result of bitter, vicious, and poisonous words, rejection penetrates deep into the soul and spirit, taking years to overcome.

Tragically, damaged souls with debilitating pain may never recover. I know a woman whose entire family, parents and siblings, took great delight in using words to abuse, belittle, crush, humiliate, and shame her from the time she was a toddler. This abuse carried over to school where classmates bullied her. Why she didn't run away or commit suicide still surprises me. Because this occurred before child services and counselors became a normal part of society, she suffered the cruelty with no recourse. Over the years, the bruising she endured perverted the destiny God designed for her. She is one of multitudes with lives shattered by the perverse spirit.

At this juncture, brutal memories may be assaulting you due to vicious, mean-spirited words. Perhaps someone thrust daggers into your soul even today. Whatever the reason, we always find our healing in the presence of God:

Abba Father, we come before you today, hearts aching. We cry out with groanings too deep for words. Only you, our Innermost Sanctuary, can heal the festering wounds of vicious and cruel words. We come before your throne of grace, vulnerable and naked, trusting the Shepherd of our souls. Pour the balm of Gilead over us. Bind up our broken hearts. Let your healing virtue flow into the depths of our beings and make us whole.

Lord, we choose to forgive each one who used their words as weapons against us. They too have wounded souls, and we ask you to heal them as well. What the enemy has meant for destruction, Almighty God, we ask you to turn it around and bring great good. We bless you, Lord, in Jesus' name. Amen.

Take time to let this prayer permeate your entire being. While our precious Savior ministers His healing, you will find rest for your weary soul.

Just Zip It Up!

How many times do you end up with strife in your home due to words turned every which way? How much division comes in your relationships because words end up contrary to what you want to say? How often do your plans get turned around because of mixed up words? I cannot tell you how many times I wish I had kept quiet, especially after I committed my life to the Lord.

Until then, I didn't think about the effects of my words, only my feelings. It's no wonder God cautions us with King Solomon's treasures in Proverbs 10:19, "In the multitude of words sin is not lacking, but he who restrains his lips is wise," and in Proverbs 4:24, "Put away from you a deceitful mouth, and put *perverse* lips far from you." More nuggets of wisdom emphasize the power of our words. Proverbs 18:21 says, "Death and life are in the power of the tongue, and those who love it will eat its fruit," while Proverbs 6:2 states, "You are snared by the words of your mouth; you are taken by the words of your mouth." Jesus confirmed this in Matthew 12:37, "For by your words you will be justified, and by your words you will be condemned."

Using this powerful truth, God literally blinded me with His Word to brand it into my entire being. Years ago as a hungry baby Christian, I diligently took time in the morning for prayer and devotions. Some teaching I received encouraged reading a chapter of Proverbs corresponding to the day. I faithfully incorporated this into my little routine, and little, by the way, is key. I taught in the public schools and didn't have many spare minutes before heading out the door. My prayer time consisted of worship, confession of any sins, thanking God for all His blessings, and praying for others. Pride radiated when I managed to squeeze in Proverbs and still keep it under five minutes.

During this season of my life, disappointment and anger boiled inside me with my husband's seemingly apparent failings. One October afternoon I sought counsel from my pastor. He encouraged me to look for the good things in my husband. Not what I wanted to hear. The following Saturday morning at our church's women's retreat, my pastor's wife shared about husbands.

Good! She's going to nail these so-called men of God! Catching me completely off-guard, she encouraged us to pray for our husbands because of the heavy responsibility God placed on them to care for their wives and children. Not what I wanted to hear.

What did I want? Someone to tell my husband to straighten up. Instead, God wanted *me* to straighten up. From His perspective, I evidently didn't get the message. I went to bed that night with no idea a special delivery from heaven was scheduled to rock my world in the morning.

Come Sunday, an hour before church, I sat on the couch doing my prayer routine. Whipping through my list in good time, I opened my Bible to finish with Proverbs 14. I read the first verse, "The wise woman builds her house, but the foolish pulls it down with her hands."

At the last word, a brilliant white light, brighter than a laser, flew up from the Bible, hit me in the face so hard my neck snapped back. Millions of dazzling white dots swirled around my head, blinding me. Time froze.

In reality, the blindness lasted mere seconds. But the truth? A lifetime. I was the foolish woman, pulling down my husband, and consequently, my house. Instead of bolstering his confidence and encouraging him, I used my words to tear him down. I quickly repented, asked God to forgive me, and prayed for wisdom to help me in the days ahead. Through a divine correction, the intense illumination of the Word taught me a lesson I have never forgotten.

Even though the time to walk out the revelation didn't happen overnight, the truth went deep into my spirit. Those seeds now flourish in my life. Words have power, for good and for evil. Today, I choose God's wisdom over an open door for a perverse spirit to slither in and short circuit my destiny. I hope you lay hold of this truth for yourself as well. Come with me to the throne of grace to lift our voices together:

Oh God in heaven, our hearts grieve from words we have sent as arrows, damaging others. We cry out as Paul did, "Who can save our wretched souls?" And our answer is the same, "Only Jesus, our Messiah, our Lord." Please forgive us, God, as we cry out for mercy. Wash us with the precious blood of Jesus, and through His blood, bring healing to those we have wounded.

Holy Spirit, we ask for your words to impart grace, not cruelty, and to bring refreshing life, not crushing bondage. We want our speech to be full of truth, wrapped in your unfailing love. Let our words be apples of gold in settings of silver.

Father, please rain down mercy and grace. Soothe our troubled souls as only you can. Hide us under the shadow of your wing and let your blanket of peace cover us. Thank you again, Lord, for straightening crooked places and bringing us to the place where we radiate your light in the dark, in Jesus' name. Amen.

You may need more time to contemplate the power of your words. Take it. Talk to the One whose words set the worlds in motion. He knows just what to say.

Let's See How Far We Can Stretch Today!

We have more to uncover. Are you ready to look at another secret? Four Hebrew words and one Greek word carry the concept of *stretch and distort*.[18] Scripture bears this out. In Acts 13, Elymas, the false prophet and sorcerer, certainly had his own agenda—maintaining his power and position with the proconsul.

To summarize, at a point during the travels of Paul and Barnabas, the two landed on the island of Paphos. They met Elymas who was with the proconsul, Sergius Paulus. The proconsul wanted to hear the apostle speak; Elymas tried to keep him from the inspired words of God with distortion. Paul saw through this scheme and confronted him, saying, ". . . will you not cease *perverting* the straight ways of the Lord?" Although this story ended on a good note (the proconsul believed and the false prophet was judged), the perverse spirit often succeeds in distorting the truth, keeping people in the dark, remaining undiscovered.

Reflect on the times truth gets stretched or distorted. If you're drawing a blank, think about the last advertisements or commercials you noticed. Regardless of the domain, be it sports, food, cars, politics, or others, the real motive behind them is to further someone's agenda. To accomplish the task, stretching or distorting the truth often achieves the goal. Spin masters with hidden schemes perform at their heights of glory, cajoling the reader or viewer to buy into their product with sometimes deceptive promises.

And speaking of being kept in the dark, how about shedding light in areas of our own lives where we stretch and distort the truth? Of course, we wouldn't do that. Or would we? Does the term *exaggeration* help dispel any lingering shadows? What an easy snare to fall prey to, considering the need for approval we eagerly covet and the nagging insecurity of our damaged souls.

To overcome, we exaggerate—the weather, the traffic, the shopping crowds; our children's successes, our overworked lives, our overbearing relatives. Our exaggeration continues in the church—the pastor's message, the worship music, the size of the youth group; our tithes and offerings, our missionary support, our community outreach. What don't we exaggerate? We look no different than the world. We just try to package ours better.

Truth has become a valuable commodity in the times we live. Yet, if we cultivate our relationship with the Spirit of Truth, who lives on the inside of us, our words will carry power and grace to change not just hearts, but nations. It's time to bring an end to the exaggeration, turn our ammunition of truth against the perverse spirit, and stop him in his tracks:

Lord, you are the Father of Lights, and we ask for your light to shine in our darkness. Bring healing and wholeness to our souls. Remind us that we find our security in you, our souls are anchored to you, and our hope rests in you.

Abba Father, we ask forgiveness for every time we stretched, distorted, and exaggerated the truth. We repent and purpose to change the way we think. We cry out as David did; we desire truth in our inward parts. Make the crooked places straight in our hearts, our minds, our bodies.

Father of Mercies, let your truth become our plumb line as we walk the Highway of Holiness, our hearts fixed on you. Holy Spirit, thank you for leading and guiding us into the light of truth. Convict us every time we stray from Truth, Jesus Christ. Bring us back into alignment with the Living Word. Deliver us with your truth to live and walk and breathe your freedom. Let the light within us serve as beacons to lead others out of darkness. We worship you, in Jesus' name. Amen.

Spend a few minutes, or even hours, meditating on Truth—the truth of who He is, who He is in us, and who we are in Him. You won't regret it.

Before we leave this section, let's check out another area often stretched—time. One word for perverse in Hebrew carries the idea of *prolonging*.[19] I'm not talking about the timing of the Lord or waiting on God, both important in our walk with Him. I'm referring to situations dragging on for months or desires becoming the dangling carrot just out of grasp. I believe this results from a perverse spirit prolonging time.

Unfortunately, I have first-hand experience of this particular manifestation. The dangling carrot? My marriage. From the moment we returned from our honeymoon, my husband threatened to divorce me. Because of my own insecurities and bondages, the torment persisted, year after year, day in and day out. The bruising my spirit endured left a crushing burden, destroying me on the inside.

About a year and a half after my divorce, I attended evangelistic meetings in another city. During a time of worship, God revealed a picture of me:

I am in a boxing match, sitting in my corner of the ring. I see my heart outside my body, bruised and bloodied. Alone and exhausted, my head rolls side-to-side. No one comes to offer any support, not even a drink of water. Although I have no strength to go on, I know the match will continue.

The Lord gave me this comparison to highlight my wounded emotional state. Present-day boxers fight three-minute rounds with a conclusion. My rounds? Never-ending, constant pummeling. The blows? Threatening words slamming into me over and over with no respite.

The subtle tactic of the perverse spirit to prolong and stretch time assaults us relentlessly. We give up, harden our hearts, and turn bitter toward God. As a matter of fact, Scripture is well aware of the effects of prolonged delays. Proverbs 13:12 says, "Hope deferred makes the heart sick . . ." Even our physical bodies suffer when dreams and desires remain unfulfilled, a scenario played out repeatedly.

While God ministered healing to my battered spirit in those meetings, He also brought powerful truths to light. Years of torment with no end in sight is not God. Your heart's desire dangled in front of you is not God. Though I intended to continue with another view of stretching, I have a sense the Lord wants to minister to those in these situations:

Almighty God, we praise and bless your holy name. You are the Ancient of Days, Wisdom from on high, the Author and Finisher of our faith. You know the end from the beginning, and nothing remains hidden from you. You created time and bestowed it upon us as a gift. Yet the enemy of our souls uses time to hurl false accusations toward you. Forgive us, Lord, for doubting you, for maligning who you are, for thinking and believing the worst about you. Rain down mercy on our souls. Renew a right spirit within us and cleanse us with the blood of Jesus. When we fall, remind us how you faithfully perfect all things concerning us.

I now stand in the gap and lift up every person whose circumstances have been prolonged by the enemy, whose hearts are bruised, battered, and even sickened because of the dangled carrot. In the authority of Jesus' name, I command you, perverse spirit, to stop and cease in your maneuvers. I break your assignment to prolong and delay. I decree and declare it is finished. You cannot succeed in perverting the timing of God. I declare the Lordship of Jesus Christ over this situation, and I thank you, Lord, for bringing about your desired end.

Merciful Father, I ask you to pour the balm of Gilead over damaged souls. Bind up wounds and heal broken hearts. Let their strength be renewed and refreshed by you in the waiting so they can mount up with eagles' wings and soar on your wind, in Jesus' name. Amen.

You may need to bask in His love for a time. I hope you do. Remember, time is not your enemy. You really can wait on the Lord. Really.

Who Decided Funhouse Mirrors Were Fun?

Do you remember passing by funhouse mirrors at carnivals? They purposely distort images, and in fact, present false pictures to those who look in them, all for a few bucks and some cheap laughs. In a sense, funhouse mirrors help us understand one of the motives of the perverse spirit—to distort how we view life. We now see how he stretches and distorts truth  and time. An area few, if any, connect to this wily serpent relates to finances. Do you ever hope money *stretches* until the end of the month or groceries *stretch* until payday? Before we get excited and blame satan for our own poor financial management, we need to understand how he uses the perverse spirit against our prosperity.

In the definitions of distorted or stretched in Hebrew, one specific meaning contains the concept of *something that's false.*[20] Therein lies the twisted thinking resulting in our financial bondage: False images of wealth, riches, and abundance. Nowhere in Scripture does this truth stand out more than in Revelation 3:17 when the apostle John warned the lukewarm Laodiceans. These believers had said, "I am rich, have become wealthy, and have need of nothing." Jesus bluntly told them they were "wretched, miserable, poor, blind, and naked." How did  they get that way? I believe a perverse spirit distorted their thinking, leading them to a false image, based on wealth and riches.

Unfortunately, Christians today row the same boat. Jobs, investment portfolios, savings accounts, inheritances, and more, keep believers smug in their religious houses, their future assured. After all, why worry? However, God's Word is straightforward with regard to trusting riches, a foolish and dangerous path. Look at this partial list of pitfalls:

Those who trust in their wealth and boast in the multitude of their riches, none of them can by any means redeem his brother, nor give to God a ransom for him—for the redemption of their souls is costly . . . (Ps. 49:6–8a)

Why do you boast in evil, O mighty man? . . . Your tongue devises destruction, like a sharp razor working deceitfully. You love evil more than good, lying rather than speaking righteousness. God shall likewise destroy you forever . . . Here is the man who did not make God his strength, but trusted in the abundance of his riches . . . (Ps. 52:1, 5, 7)

If riches increase, do not set your heart on them. (Ps. 62:10b)

He who trusts in his riches will fall . . . (Prov. 11:28a)

Will you set your eyes on that which is not? For riches certainly make themselves wings; they fly away like an eagle . . . (Prov. 23:5)

These Scriptures unequivocally describe the results of trusting in riches—false images of security, leading to failure. In fact, God warns us in Deuteronomy 8:17 to not forget the Lord when we achieve success and prosperity. Otherwise, we will say, along with the Israelites, "My power and the might of my hand have gained me this wealth." Doesn't this sound familiar? Revelation 3 perhaps? The Laodicean church perhaps? To quote it again, "I am rich, have become wealthy, and have need of nothing."

False perverted thinking, one of the easiest, yet most deceptive, methods satan employs, keeps Christians in financial bondage without their knowledge. Wealth used improperly and with wrong motives puts believers in chains. Jesus warned his followers about the pitfalls of financial bondage. In Mark 4, He cautioned the disciples not to let the deceitfulness of riches choke out the Word of God in their lives. After a discussion with the rich young ruler in Matthew 19, He described the difficult path the wealthy encounter trying to enter the kingdom of heaven. His comments left the disciples in utter shock. Their understanding of salvation included money.

While we live in a different millennium, human nature remains the same. People still attempt to buy their way to heaven. But God's plan of salvation never depends on the size of our bank accounts. Lest we forget, the Bible emphatically states in Ephesians 2:8–9 that we receive salvation by grace through faith and not of any works, including our checking accounts.

This is not to say God doesn't want His people to prosper. Quite the contrary. In Deuteronomy 8:18, the Great I AM laid out the divine purpose of wealth to His people before they went into the Promised Land, "And you shall remember the LORD your God, for it is He who gives you power to get wealth, that He may establish His covenant . . ." A number of Scriptures refer to riches coming from the hand of God:

Praise the LORD! Blessed is the man who fears the LORD, who delights greatly in His commandments . . . Wealth and riches will be in his house, and his righteousness endures forever. (Ps. 112:1, 3)

By humility and the fear of the LORD are riches and honor and life. (Prov. 22:4)

The blessing of the LORD makes one rich, and He adds no sorrow with it. (Prov. 10:22)

. . . but those who seek the LORD lack no good thing. (Ps. 34:10b NIV)

Let the LORD be magnified, who has pleasure in the prosperity of His servant. (Ps. 35:27)

And God is able to make all grace abound toward you, that you, always having all sufficiency in all things, may have an abundance for every good work. (2 Cor. 9:8–9)

And these are only a smattering of the verses referring to God's kingdom finances.

We need to understand this one thing: **God wants us to prosper**. He is for us, not against us. He doesn't try to withhold prosperity from us. He willingly pours out of His treasure purse, and not just a little bit. All the gold and silver and the cattle on a thousand hills belong to Him. He looks for ways to bless us, spiritually and financially. Remember, Jesus fed thousands with two fish and five loaves of bread. God's mindset regarding finances is multiplication, not stretching. He doesn't sit on His throne wondering if He has enough gold to pave the streets. In Genesis 17:1, God refers to Himself as El-Shaddai, the All-Sufficient One, the Mighty Breasted One.[21] In Genesis 22:14, Abraham calls Him Jehovah Jireh, the God Who Will See To It.[22] This God is our God. The One who knows no lack, only abundance.

Yet, by robbing God's children, the perverse spirit robs God from fulfilling His desire to exponentially multiply kingdom finances. God pursues sons and daughters who move in wisdom, integrity, obedience, and faith when it comes to financial prosperity. Most Christians sincerely desire to walk in these attributes.

However, the path to prosperity can present many obstacles to overcome, such as generational curses, inner vows, poverty spirits, and poor money management skills. Still, one of the most cunning culprits, the perverse spirit, cons believers into looking at their finances through funhouse mirrors. This produces distorted and false images of God's purposes for finances, which, again, is to establish His covenant in the earth; which is the Great Commission: Go ye into all the world, preach the gospel, make disciples . . . (Matthew 28:19–20). Instead, they see money as their security; in other words, their salvation. What can't they see? The burdensome chains weighing them down. The bottom line? The thief doesn't care how he steals, kills, and destroys as long as he gets the job done. Perverting the way believers view finances makes an effective tool for him.

I don't know where you stand with your finances. Maybe you are one of God's trusted stewards, moving in abundance. If so, thank God, thank God we have saints who pay the price and walk in obedience to God. May He continue to pour out more of His treasure purse so His covenant continues to be established in the earth. For those of us who look in the funhouse mirrors and see false images of our prosperity, we can come before our heavenly Father and ask for truth from the Spirit of Truth:

Oh God, you are awesome in splendor, majestic in beauty. We stand before you in fear and trembling. For along with our fathers and forefathers, we have sinned against you. We lifted another idol to save us. We took the resources you entrusted to us and distorted your divine purposes for them. Instead of trusting you, we built up financial walls to rescue us. We come before you now, condemned and guilty of perverting financial blessings from your hand. We see how truly wretched, miserable, poor, blind, and naked we are. Jesus, we ask for refining fire to purge the dross out of us, for white garments of holiness to clothe our nakedness, and for eye salve to anoint our eyes so we see with heaven's perspective.

Father, forgive us for our ignorance and arrogance. Cleanse us with the mighty blood of Jesus. We renounce the perverted patterns that set us on a path away from you. We tear down the fraudulent walls we built up. We smash the false images we created. We bind the perverse spirit from our finances and break all assignments against them. As we declare Jesus Lord over them, we determine to establish our finances on your Word and use our wealth to accomplish your purposes. Lord, you are the God of Abundance, Jehovah-Jireh, our Exceedingly Great Reward. Hallelujah, hallelujah to the Great I AM! We praise and bless you, in Jesus' name. Amen.

Glory to God! Abandon yourself in worship to the Living God. Enjoy what He's doing in your life and walk in expectancy because He's a good God!

Knowing how the enemy of our souls distorts images of finances, we can more easily discern other views coming from funhouse mirrors. As

Christians, we know the Bible declares us to be new creations. Yet, how many believers walk through their days with distorted images of themselves due to painful childhoods? We view life through past mistakes and failures instead of through the cross and the blood Jesus shed to bring us into wholeness.

According to Scripture, we need to behold the glory of the Lord to be transformed into His image. Second Corinthians 3:18 puts it this way, "But we all, with unveiled face, beholding as in a mirror the glory of the Lord, are being transformed into the same image from glory to glory, just as by the Spirit of the Lord." If we don't gaze on the image of Jesus, who do we look at, or rather, look up to? Who do we aspire to become? For worldly pursuits, we elevate the hottest movie stars, athletes, or singers to the high places in our lives to emulate them. Trying to be spiritual, we look for the most anointed prophet, pastor, or worship leader to put on a pedestal.

With either choice, we put weak, carnal men and women just like us in the place only fit for One greater than us, holier than us, purer than us. If we don't put someone else in the high place, we set ourselves up as the most holy. Rather than a reflection of Jesus to a lost and dying world, we present distorted images from the funhouse mirrors courtesy of the perverse spirit. And we wonder why the sinner, the heathen, the backslidden tune out, turn off, and turn away.

In addition to the perverted views we have of ourselves, we end up with twisted views of God—who He is, what He thinks of us, what He expects of us. We look at Him through our woundedness and lower Him to our level. We expect God to act and think like we do. Ironically, most of us aren't happy with God because we think He's just like us. Since we carry within us a desire and need to worship someone, once we pull Almighty God down to our level, we're forced to put somebody on the high place. Our options? Another person or ourselves.

Consequently, we find ourselves walking in idolatry. Like a well-known fallen angel, we turn the worship of God to ourselves. Isaiah recorded Lucifer's boasts in chapter 14:13–14, "I will ascend into heaven, I will exalt my throne above the stars of God; I will also sit on the mount of the congregation on the farthest sides of the north; I will ascend above the heights of the clouds, I will be like the Most High." While we would never openly boast like Lucifer, our motives mirror his.

Today the perverse spirit uses this prime method of operation in the church—twisting the worship of God to the worship of man. When that happens, somebody is going to crash and burn. Stories abound of Christian leaders who fall into various sins, be it adultery, alcoholism, or addictions. We have all read reports of well-known pastors who succumbed to the adulation surrounding them, destroying families and churches.

Moreover, the perverse spirit employs a much more insidious tactic involving the physical body and funhouse mirrors. Countless young people, particularly girls, find themselves in bondage to eating disorders.[23] Without going into the various causes and resulting effects of anorexia and bulimia, suffice it to say that a perverse spirit carefully twists the thinking of his victims when they look in a mirror. Instead of seeing rib cages and shoulder blades sticking out like malnourished children in third-world countries, they see and hear, "You're too fat." Without divine and medical intervention, death can loom in the crisis. Another family may find itself sitting in a memorial service because a loved one succumbed to the twisted lies of the perverse spirit.

Janice* came face-to-face with this concerning Katie, her youngest. Growing up, her two girls developed completely different personalities. One clear difference dealt with mealtime. Maribeth, her oldest, enjoyed food and helped set the table just to eat sooner. On the other hand, when Janice served lunch or dinner, she had to call Katie several times to come to the table. At some point, Janice realized this didn't stem from rebellion, but from a disinterest in food. What didn't she realize? How the enemy planned to use this to destroy her daughter.

One December, a well-known evangelist held meetings in another town. Janice picked up a friend, stopped at the girls' favorite fast food place to grab their supper, and headed down the interstate. Along the way, she reminded her girls to eat. Throughout the drive, the four passed the time chatting and praying, with a few giggles along the way. Once at the meeting, they fully enjoyed the message and ministry, glad they made the trip, even in the dead of winter.

After reaching their hotel room around eleven o'clock, they hurried into jammies. Katie complained of a headache and dizziness. Janice and her friend started to pray. Maribeth interrupted them, "Momma, Katie didn't eat her supper."

Shocked, Janice questioned her second born. Katie admitted she hadn't eaten any of it. Janice pulled out some snacks to get food in her daughter's tummy, but she refused. The three of them spent several minutes convincing Katie to eat. When she finally agreed, she felt better after a few munchies.

However, that's not the end of the story. A couple of months later, Janice and Katie were in the car running errands. Katie started talking about her goldfish, Glory, and asked, "Momma, do you think Glory has anorexia?" Janice managed to stay calm on the outside as the two discussed Glory's eating habits. Inside, not so much. Eating disorders, especially anorexia, did not get discussed in their home. At ten years old, Katie didn't even know the word, let alone what it meant. Janice recognized satan's scheme—to deceive her daughter into believing lies about herself, with the ultimate goal of killing her and destroying their family.

After the girls went to bed, she called a friend, and they went to war. Spiritual war! Even though they defeated the enemy that night, his inroad into Katie had taken hold. For years, Janice maintained a watchful diligence to keep him at bay. Not until the summer Katie turned sixteen did the threat end, and Janice danced a victory jig, praising God!

On the other hand, contrary to those wasting away, funhouse mirrors become reality for the overweight. Unlike anorexic victims who can't see their emaciated bodies, they see literal rolls of flesh. When looking in a mirror, they hear the taunting voice, "You'll never lose weight. You'll always be fat. No one wants you." As with all eating disorders, obesity carries its own set of health problems and private agony, sometimes with devastating results.

I have friends who struggle with it, some since childhood. Even though they make jokes or have smart comebacks regarding their sizes, their secret torment adds more weight to the images they see in the looking glass.

Yet in the midst of the suffering, the key is not to look outward to other people or inward to ourselves. The writer of Hebrews underscored this truth when he exhorted fellow believers to look to Jesus, the Author and Finisher of our faith, the one who paid the price to sit on the throne of our hearts (12:2). According to Colossians 3:3, our position is to be hidden in Christ so when a man or woman of the world looks at us, they see Him. Only by staying in Christ, can we be free from the past and experience true freedom, leading us into our destinies. Walking in our liberty, we can, in turn, lead others into theirs.

Before leaving this section, I want to share an experience demonstrating the idea of funhouse mirrors. During the worship time of a conference I attended several years ago, God gave me a vision:

Jesus walks down a sidewalk. He is huge! Every person He encounters must go into Him. No one can get around Him, over Him, or under Him. The only way forward is to go into Jesus. As I walk toward Him, I notice a man to my left. We both step into Jesus at the same time. Once inside, I realize I have complete freedom to do whatever I want. I do somersaults, back flips, and cartwheels. The joy is exhilarating! No limitations exist inside Him. All hindrances, bondages, and restrictions disappear. I then see the other man. Instead of staying inside, he walks out the back of Jesus. At the point he breaks out, I see his silhouette. It looks like the outline of a comic strip character smashing through a wall. The man continues down the sidewalk, his entire body distorted, just as if he collided into a wall. I stay inside Jesus and continue my gymnastics.

This is a picture of the future. All will have an encounter with Jesus. None will be exempt. In choosing to remain in Christ when this event takes place, full liberty awaits. Choosing to step out of Jesus, a distorted life looms ahead, one without freedom, only bondage to funhouse images. The choice is ours. Oh, God, have mercy on us!

Father, you are perfection. No one comes close to your ultimate holiness, your magnificent glory. Because of your indescribable love, you chose to make us like you. And when we chose rebellion, you sent Jesus so we could see what you looked like. And when we crucified Him, you sent the very essence of who you are through Holy Spirit to live on the inside of us.

God, we are weary beyond weary of funhouse mirror images mocking us. We long to see ourselves the way you do. Forgive us for putting others on the highest place in our hearts. Lord, we renounce every form of idolatry. We cast down every idol. We tear down the high places we established out of our wounds and weaknesses. We smash the funhouse mirrors that twisted our views of ourselves, others, and you. We trust you, Father, to heal and restore our souls.

Once again, we declare you, Jesus, Lord over our lives. We exalt you above every other name. We bow before you, the very image of heaven. You are glorious in majesty, and we worship you. Above all, we want to behold you, the Lover of our every breath, as we move and live and have our being in you and you alone, in your holy name we pray. Amen.

According to Scripture, the only image we need to behold is the glory of the Lord. Throw out your funhouse mirrors and take time to feast on His glory. When you finish, if you ever do, you might not recognize yourself.

Tummy Troubles

I know I'm supposed to wait until the beginning of the chapter to ask questions, but I had to jump in at this point. What on earth does a perverse spirit have to do with a stomach-ache? This is not rocket science. If you stuff yourself with pizza and buffalo wings, you're gonna get heartburn. Up to this point, you've been convincing me the perverse spirit is real and probably lurking around me somewhere. But a stomachache? I don't think so. A couple of antacids should take care of the problem, right?

Wrong. Remember, the meanings for perverse include *to knot* or *distort*[24] and *to stretch*.[25] Others mean *to twist*[26] and *to swell up*.[27] To shed light on this particular aspect of the perverse spirit, I want to share what happened to Rebekah. First, a little biology. In adults, the digestive tract is nearly thirty feet long from start to finish. Numerous folds and creases occur naturally inside our bodies to accomplish the incredible feat of digesting the food we eat. Babies' intestines are under-developed, hence, the need to grow from milk to solid foods. In addition, as any parent knows, their tummies get easily upset due to gas and bloating. For the most part, adults don't have major problems moving things along; babies, though, need those gentle, firm taps on the back to settle their tummies and keep them happy.

Unfortunately, this didn't happen for Rebekah. If she didn't get rid of the gas quickly, she had a full-blown tummy ache lasting for hours. Her little belly twisted and knotted, and she contorted herself trying to alleviate the pain. One night, at the end of my proverbial rope, I decided to come against a perverse spirit. I honestly didn't think it would work. Without anything to lose, except another long night with a crying baby, I started to pray.

"In Jesus' name, I bind you, perverse spirit, from Rebekah, and I command you to leave her body. You have no authority over her. She's my daughter, and she's covered with the blood of Jesus. I demand every knot and kink to come loose from her tummy.

"Now, Rebekah, I call your spirit to come up to your place of peace in Jesus. You'll feel so much better, sweetheart. Come up to your peace."

Lo and behold, she experienced some relief almost immediately. Within minutes, she was back to her sweet, happy self. "Thank you, God, thank you," I kept repeating, stunned by this turn of events. I continued thanking Him until I finally went to bed.

After that night, when tummy troubles clamored for attention, I bound up a perverse spirit and commanded those knots, kinks, and twists to be loosed. Sometimes her distress lasted a long time, but the more I understood my authority in Christ, the sooner Rebekah experienced relief.

A number of years later, I attended a School of Revival in Boston. One Sunday morning during my turn at nursery duty, a baby boy started crying.

When I picked him up, I put my hand on his tummy and felt knots and kinks. Quietly, I commanded them to be loosed from him and bound the perverse spirit. I then called for his spirit to come up to his peace in Jesus. Within minutes, he calmed down and took a nap.

The most amazing part of the story involved the mother. Every service this little boy's nursery number lit up in the sanctuary at least twice because no one managed to stop his crying. However, this particular morning, the mother worried so much when his number didn't light up that she came back to check on him. She didn't know what to think when she saw him sleeping. Later, he woke up a happy little camper.

The question you're probably asking is, "Does this mean every bit of indigestion is caused by the perverse spirit?" Of course not. Still, this spirit attacks our bodies as well as our minds. Due to the design of the digestive tract, with its natural twists and turns, this organ presents an easy target for the perverse spirit to zero in on and create pain. Remember, satan's purpose is to steal, kill, and destroy, and he doesn't care how he does it.

For those of you with infants and toddlers who have tummy troubles, you can pray the way I did for Rebekah. Bind the perverse spirit in Jesus' name. Command every knot, kink, and twist to be loosed. Speak to the spirit of your child to come up to his peace in Jesus. Why peace? For several reasons: 1) Peace is a weapon. Romans 16:20 states the God of peace crushes satan under our feet. 2) The Hebrew meaning for peace is *to be completed*; in other words, *nothing missing, nothing broken, everything made whole*.[28] Whatever is amiss in your child's digestive tract clearly needs to be made whole. 3) Jesus spoke, "Peace, be still," and the storm instantly calmed. You may not be out on a blustery lake in the middle of the night, but the storm in your house needs to be stilled.

While I'm not a physician and would never encourage you to not seek medical treatment, I know the power of prayer. Besides, what have you got to lose except another sleepless night? (A note for adults: You can pray this for yourselves as well. It certainly won't hurt, and just might help.)

Work, Work, Work

Work. Say it and countless images play across the imagination: Some good, some not so good, some bad, some really, really bad. More often than not, the really, really bad images cause us to recoil from work and look forward to the end of the day, the end of the week, the beginning of vacation, or the start of retirement just so we don't have to work.

What do our jobs have to do with a perverse spirit? More than you think. Two Hebrew words have definitions connected to work. One means *to toil,*[29] and its root states *to work severely with irksomeness.*[30] The other is defined as *misemployment*[31] and comes from a word meaning *a rut or worn track or path.*[32]

While employment issues can arise from changes in management or company policy, situations abound where the perverse spirit works behind the scenes. For two living, breathing examples, we can look at Pete* and Rose, both caught in the trap of the perverse spirit in their work lives.

In Pete's case, he struggles to find the right job. He tries numerous positions, all ending in failure. He either gets fired or he quits. Even in the positions he has held, he is unhappy, and his fellow employees find it difficult to work with him. He doesn't like the work, doesn't like his coworkers, doesn't like his boss. This man finds fault with everyone and everything while taking no responsibility for himself. Despised by those he works with, he lives out the truth found in Proverbs 12:8, "But he who is of a *perverse* heart will be despised."

Alienated in the workforce, when Pete applies for jobs, employers don't consider him. Known as a high-risk job candidate, his reputation precedes him as Proverbs 10:9 demonstrates, "He who walks with integrity walks securely, but he who *perverts* his ways will become known." Pete does not walk with integrity. He uses things, people, and God to achieve his goals. He twists the truth to fit his own agenda, then laments the rut he can't get out of. A perfect rut perfectly designed by the perverse spirit.

Then there's Rose, a college student, who wants out of her miserable job. She finds another position with a company willing to work with her class schedule. By the end of the first week, Rose sees trouble on the once promising horizon. Her supervisor ignores the assurances made during the interview regarding her classes, and the other employees treat her as an outsider. Her misemployment, via the perverse spirit, leads to tears and sleepless nights.

Both Pete and Rose, and others like them, will develop crooked paths regarding employment. Can they avoid these twisted trails? With powerfully anointed prayers, a divine intervention can give them a breakthrough over the perverse spirit in their lives.

We can look at another aspect of the root word for *toil*: *Wearying effort; worry of body or mind; misery.*[33] This insidious trait takes particular aim against those in ministry. Testimonies abound of ministers exhausted, ready to walk away from their calling. Unfortunately, countless numbers succumb to the ploys of the perverse spirit in his relentless attack against leaders in the body of Christ. Various studies show hundreds of pastors leaving the ministry.[34] What a tragic end to the calling of God!

Let's get personal. Do you find yourself in a rut, going nowhere, spinning wheels like a rat on a tread wheel? Maybe you're in a ministry position and bone-weary with the work. Miserable is the nicest way to describe it. Or do you have an irritating job and want to be anywhere but there. How many coworkers are difficult to work with? Cranky, irritable, nothing good to say about anything, especially their jobs? Or do you fit the description of the cranky, irritable employee despised by others? Ouch!

Clearly, working severely, stuck in a rut, bone-weary with work, or despised by your coworkers does not bring to mind "life, liberty, and the pursuit of happiness." When the founding fathers penned those words in the Declaration of Independence, they knew these ideas came from God. Scripture, indeed, supports what they wrote centuries ago:

The labor of the righteous leads to life . . . (Prov. 10:16a)

And let the beauty of the LORD our God be upon us, and establish the work of our hands for us; yes, establish the work of our hands. (Ps. 90:17)

For He repays man according to his work, and makes man to find a reward according to his way. Surely God will never do wickedly, nor will the Almighty *pervert* justice. (Job 34:11–12)

What profit has the worker from that in which he labors? . . . He [God] has made everything beautiful in its time. Also He has put eternity in their hearts . . . I know that nothing is better for them than to rejoice, and to do good in their lives, and also that every man should eat and drink and enjoy the good of all his labor—it is the gift of God. (Eccl. 3:9, 11a, 12–13)

As for every man to whom God has given riches and wealth, and given him power to eat of it, to receive his heritage and rejoice in his labor—this is the gift of God. For he will not dwell unduly on the days of his life, because God keeps him busy with the joy of his heart. (Eccl. 5:19–20)

Look to yourselves, that we do not lose those things we worked for, but that we may receive a full reward. (2 John 8)

God makes it clear He wants us to enjoy our work and be blessed in it.

Even more, His plan for work intended to bring us into communion with Him. Remember, He planted the garden in Eden and put Adam there to tend it. The King James Version states in Genesis 2:15, "And the LORD God took the man, and put him into the garden of Eden to dress it and to keep it." Since Eden displayed perfection, we can assume the garden mirrored its flawlessness. No thorns, no thistles, no boll weevils, no locusts; only beauty enhanced even more when God walked through it during the cool of the day. Although things changed drastically the moment Adam sinned, God's original plan remains the same—find joy in the work of our hands.

If you moaned and groaned reading this section, the perverse spirit has more than likely slithered in and out of your employment, wreaking havoc.

It's what he likes to do best, derail destinies. But we can ask for help to get our lives back on track:

Holy God, forgive us for going our own way and relying on our own strength. We trusted in our knowledge and abilities with no regard of your plans for us. We tried to make something of ourselves and forgot you in the process. We have lost our joy and our purpose in life. We're in a rut we can't get out of. Please rescue us and deliver us from bondage. Set us on the rock higher than us, our Savior and King, Jesus.

You have a destiny for us to fulfill, Lord, and we cannot do it without you. Lead us and guide us; teach us the way we should go. Open doors no man can close, and close doors no man can open. Continue to straighten the crooked places. Father, we forgive those who turned our jobs into torment. Touch their lives and bring them into your freedom.

Now in the mighty name of Jesus, we take authority over you, satan. We bind the perverse spirit from our employment and break his assignment over our work. We declare no weapon formed against us shall prosper and every tongue rising in judgment against us is condemned. This is our inheritance, and our righteousness is found in our Eternal God.

Father, thank you for wisdom and understanding to help us make choices birthed from your heart. Because you establish the work of our hands, we decree that we are fruitful and profitable for the sake of your kingdom. Thank you, Lord, for keeping us busy with the joy of our hearts. We praise and bless you, our Mighty Redeemer, in Jesus' name. Amen.

Take time to worship the God of your soul. He is worthy and honorable. He loves you with an everlasting love, and forever and always thinks the absolute best of you and for you.

Busy As a Bee

Busy as a bee. Hmmm. How about busy as a busybody? We find a rather unusual treasure in the same Greek word for *misemployment*. While sharing a meaning with *meddlesome*, it implies *perverse disputings*.[35] What exactly are *perverse disputings*? They occur when someone twists the truth and then argues the twisted truth *is* the truth. How does that translate into reality? A personal example. My daughters grew up without a father, the result of Christian meddling  and *perverse disputings*. How did it happen? Some Christian friends decided they knew the will of God for our marriage and hotly pursued it.

Although they anticipated the resulting turmoil and strife, they didn't expect us to divorce. Based on various conversations, or rather, *perverse disputings*, they honestly believed they, as Christian brothers and sisters, had a right to meddle. They assumed their interference would put us back together. Instead, our marriage suffered irreparable damage. We never recovered.

Christian meddling led a couple of my friends to marry the wrong men. Neither had a desire to walk down the aisle nor an attraction to the men they eventually married. Due to Christian busybodies and the pressure they exerted, including *perverse disputings,* my friends eventually said, "I do." One divorced after seven years while the other one has a marriage license without a real marriage. Unfortunately, the destinies of both women turned quite around thanks to believers working hand in glove with a perverse spirit.

What about busybodies in the church? Buzzing here, buzzing there. Always making their opinions known. Always knowing other people's business. Always having the last word. Puffed up with pride. Stirring up strife. Argumentative. *Perverse disputings*. Do some familiar faces or names come to mind? Could it be the one in the mirror? Yikes!

Perverse disputings. An interesting phrase. Remember the sections on words? Here we add another twist to the mix. Paul said in 1 Timothy 6:5 to *withdraw ourselves* from men who move in them. Sometimes walking away gives us the victory. In my situation, I did pull back from everyone meddling in my marriage. Unfortunately, it was too late. The perverse spirit at work in my husband eagerly accepted their interference, and he added his own *perverse disputings*. Shortly after, he abandoned me with a toddler and a baby on the way. Another family left in the wake of devastation due to the devious workings of a perverse spirit.

Are you a casualty of meddlesome Christians who decided their will matched God's will? Does your own family history have etchings of *perverse disputings*? If yes, you need to know your Abba Father designed perfect plans for you and left His imprint on your heart. Come, let's bow before His throne of grace:

Lord God, as the Righteous Judge, you sit in the highest place, with heaven your throne and earth your footstool. We come before you with broken hearts, asking you to forgive us for times we meddled and joined forces with the enemy in perverse disputings. Only you know the depth of suffering our words caused in the lives of others.

Father, we repent now and pray for the mind of Christ. We come in agreement with the Spirit of the Living God to stop pursuing our own agendas for other people. Cleanse us with the precious blood of Jesus. Let your grace and mercy fall like rain and restore us. We ask for healing and pray blessings on those whose destinies were twisted by our efforts. Thank you for making their crooked places straight.

Father, we also ask for healing and wholeness in the places perverse disputings left marks and scars on us. Cover every blemish and wound left by the enemy with the imprint of heaven's grace, mercy, and love. We forgive those who interfered in our lives. We bless them and pray their hearts will soften toward you.

We ask you to make straight every place the enemy has woven a crooked trail. Lead us again on paths of righteousness for your name's sake. Redeem the lost years we wandered the winding, crooked paths. Restore the joy of our salvation and let our mourning turn to dancing. We praise and bless you, our Great Redeemer, in Jesus' name. Amen.

Why don't you turn your mourning into dancing? Let the music in your soul get in your feet and dance among the stars. You won't be alone. Angels will be dancing next to you.

What's Your Hurry?

As I wrote this subtitle, I thought about how much time I have spent hurrying my way through life. Driving like a maniac across town. Dragging my girls from one store to another. Glaring at the slow cashiers. Flying down the interstate, always over the speed limit. What was I trying to accomplish? Better yet, what did I accomplish?

Down through the eons of time, God with all of His infinite wisdom, never hurried, not one time. So, why have I? I'm asking myself these questions because the next hidden treasure comes from a couple of Hebrew words meaning *to eagerly covet and rush upon*[36] and *to hurl, to rush headlong, and to be rash.*[37] I'm sure you're thinking, *Wait a minute—I thought the perverse spirit prolonged and stretched time. How can it mean the complete opposite?*

Remember, this wily serpent wants to warp the plans and purposes of God in your life, and he uses whatever works. He derails your destiny with delay tactics to keep you off track for months, sometimes years. Or he gets you to rush headlong and make rash decisions. Either way, he still accomplishes his goal. You will look back and wonder, "What was I thinking?" And the truth of the matter is, you weren't. At least you didn't have the mind of Christ, and you didn't walk in the wisdom of God. According to Job 5:13 in the King James Version, "The counsel of the *froward* [*perverse*] is carried headlong." Pushed, provoked, and prodded by the slippery serpent, you fell for his lies and deception. I know. I fell very, very hard. More than once.

Years ago, when the girls were small, I started a home craft business. In a short time, $18,000 of debt glared at me, daring me to pay it back. How did it happen? Although I prayed with a few friends, for the most part, I made rash decisions, rushing headlong into financial bondage. Even when over my head in debt, I continued swimming in dangerous waters. A pattern required a third of a yard of fabric? I left the shop with three yards. The project needed five packages of a certain item? Every package in every store ended up in my closet. The minimum order of professional cut mats for my prints called for fifty? I placed the order for five thousand. You read that right—five thousand.

Several years had passed since I did the study, and if you remember, it sat in a filing cabinet behind a closed door. Consequently, I didn't see the connection to the perverse spirit. As a result, I opened the door to the enemy, and my family suffered. Badly. For months, I had to make difficult decisions about how to use the little money available in my checking account. Did I pay the gas bill or phone bill, knowing one might be shut off? Did I buy light bulbs or manage with just one in the house and put gas in the car instead? Did I pay the collector his due or buy groceries so we had food for the week? Eviction became a scary possibility. Many times the unbearable pressure led me to the breaking point, even to a day when suicide appeared to be my only option. The Lord's faithfulness and countless prayers rescued me from that critical moment. Still, it took years to get out of the financial mess. Only with the favor of God and creative, divine intervention, did I pay off the debt without declaring bankruptcy.

About the same time my business was drowning, I met a man I believed to be my future husband. Since he lived over two thousand miles away, we began a phone fellowship. We experienced incredible prayer times, the anointing of God deeply touching us. Most importantly, he loved my girls.

As the days progressed, God seemed to confirm what I sensed the first night we met.

Though I spent many hours in prayer and tried not to push, the perverse spirit inside me eagerly coveted and rushed upon him. Still reeling from the rejection of my ex-husband and desperate for a mate, I charged headlong into the relationship. He picked this up and graciously tried to distance himself. Me? I knew I was right! I hotly pursued him. He bolted like a prize trophy dodging the hunter. With hindsight always the best instructor, I don't blame him.

In the end, I paid a heavy price. I struggled for years with trust issues concerning not just men, but God. This is exactly what our enemy wants, even rejoices over. Can we trust God? Will He do what He said He would? Did God really say . . . ? All these questions have the potential to lead us away from our destiny and send us rushing headlong on a crooked path, courtesy of the perverse spirit.

Even in practical, day-to-day matters, the enemy of our souls uses this tactic of rushing headlong, being rash, and eagerly coveting to throw us off track. Shoppers buy impulsively at the check-out. Black Friday sales lead to massive credit card debt. Sinister road rage ends in tragedy.

How often we forget God, the One who created time, doesn't hurry. On the other hand, we do. What's more, we think time belongs to the devil, and he controls the outcome. This is simply not true, and Scriptures prove otherwise:

> My times are in Your hand; deliver me from the hand of my enemies, and from those who persecute me. (Ps. 31:15)

> Wisdom and knowledge will be the stability of your times, and the strength of salvation; the fear of the LORD is His treasure. (Isa. 33:6)

> . . . Blessed be the name of God forever and ever, for wisdom and might are His. And He changes the times and seasons . . . (Dan. 2:20–21)

Time rests in God's hands, not satan's. We can trust Him not just with the calendar of our years — we can trust Him with every nanosecond of our lives.

To demonstrate this vital component in the manifestation of our destinies, the Lord gave me a prophecy:

Time Is No Longer Your Enemy

Time is no longer your enemy. Time has become your friend.
Embrace time, receive time, partner with time
because all time exists in Me, past, present, future.

Even as thyme is the necessary ingredient in stew,
so time is the necessary component of My plans and purposes on the earth.
When there seems to be a delay, it's because not enough time
has been included in My recipe, My plan.

As the chef allots just enough thyme to insure
his most excellent dish comes to perfection,
so do I need to allot enough time to bring forth My plans and purposes
to the utmost place of perfection in Me.

Even as the chef carefully adds the exact amount of thyme,
so I jealously guard the allotted time.
And because the enemy knows his time is short,
he continually harasses you to rush through, to push before My timer goes off.
Consequently, many of my plans and purposes are half-baked.
I have to start over with a new and fresh batch.

But no more, if you embrace My time and seasonings.
When the timer goes off, you will be the gourmet meal I present to the world.
Thousands upon thousands will feast with their eyes
and hunger in their souls to look like you.

And it will be because of the time you have spent
in My presence to receive healing and wholeness
for times of wounding, times of betrayal, times of fear, times of despair;
all the times the enemy plotted against you.

As they look upon you, My rich, fragrant cuisine, they will see Me
and be drawn to Me, and I will once again set My timer
to prepare another gourmet meal.[38]

Through this prophetic exhortation, we see the critical role time plays in our lives. I am not in any way discounting how the perverse spirit delays and stretches time. Still, the Bible admonishes us to wait on the Lord, which is good and right and wise:

I would have lost heart, unless I had believed that I would see the goodness of the LORD in the land of the living. Wait on the LORD; be of good courage, and He shall strengthen your heart; wait, I say, on the LORD! (Ps. 27:13–14)

Wait on the LORD and keep His way, and He shall exalt you to inherit the land . . . (Ps. 37:34a)

But those who wait on the LORD shall renew their strength; they shall mount up with wings like eagles, they shall run and not be weary, they shall walk and not faint. (Isa. 40:31)

And, yet, how often do we heed this call from our loving God, who gives us a future and a hope? Rushing headlong. Rash decisions. Eagerly coveting. All marks of the perverse spirit.

How many marks do you have? Are they hidden or still showing? Perhaps you can say, "Been there, done that, ain't never goin' back." Or do you still rush about pell-mell on the crooked road? Wherever you are, whatever path you're traveling, prayer only takes a few minutes:

Father God, you are the only wise God. Yet, instead of trusting and waiting on you, we rush off half-cocked, eagerly coveting. We grieve your heart deeply. And all for what? How often do we frustrate your grace in our lives? How many times do we stand in the way of your dreams for us? We align ourselves with the enemy and run headlong into bondage.

Lord, have mercy. Deliver us. Rescue us from our rash mistakes. Make the crooked places straight. Let your Word become our path. Let every mark become a landmark, a sign of your grace and mercy.

Father God, we humble ourselves before you and resist the perverse spirit. We break his hold over us in the mighty name of Jesus. We choose to change the way we think, and we purpose in our hearts to seek the mind of Christ. We ask for the spirit of wisdom and revelation to flood our hearts and minds. As we wait on you, Lord, renew our strength so we can soar like eagles. Thank you for your unfailing love for us and great faith in us. We are truly more than conquerors through Christ who loves us, in His holy name we pray. Amen.

Now would be the perfect time to wait on the Lord. As He refreshes and renews your strength, soar on the wings of His Spirit to glorious heights and keep company with the stars. You'll be glad you did.

Slipping and Sliding

Sometimes, the closer we get to our goals, the farther away they seem. We have no idea why or how. We just know we are going every direction but forward, and at times on the fast track to nowhere. Trust me, the perverse spirit willingly accommodates us to the place we slip and slide. How does he do it? If we look at a few Hebrew and Greek meanings, the answer might fall into our laps. Let's delve into them.

In order to get a fuller picture of this trait, we need to look at *froward*, which, if you remember, comes from the same Hebrew meaning as perverse.

Isaiah 57:17 states, ". . . he continued *frowardly* in his heart." Strong's definition here means *backsliding, frowardly, to turn back and not necessarily with the idea of returning to the starting point, to draw back, to hinder, to back off, withdraw.*[39] Another, translated *perverse* in some verses, means *to turn away or back*[40] and comes from other words meaning *separation or cessation*[41] as well as *to turn quite around or reverse.*[42]

Obviously, we understand the term *backsliding*. If you haven't slipped away from an intimate, on-fire relationship with God at some point in your life, you probably know someone who has. Proverbs 14:14 states, "The *backslider* in heart will be filled with his own ways," and Jeremiah 8:5 says, "[*Backsliders*] hold fast to deceit, they refuse to return." But backsliders don't start out that way, so how does it happen? A bird's eye view of marriage depicts a mirror image of the love relationship between Christ and the church, which Paul described in Ephesians 5. The marital bond presents the perfect place for a perverse spirit to bring about hindrances leading a husband and wife to withdraw from each other, turn quite around, and eventually separate and divorce.

A young couple, Sam* and Denise, deeply love each other. The two work through trials and come out stronger on the other side. All appears well. At some point on their journey, the fire of their first love begins to wane. Perhaps the busyness of life gets in the way. Too much pressure at work. Too much pressure at home. Not to mention all the activities the children have: Music lessons, ball practice, drama rehearsals, some at the same time!

Furthermore, distractions pull their attention from each other: TVs, cell phones, computers. All scream for the affections Sam and Denise once had for each other. Instead of phrases of endearment, careless barbs pierce their souls. Other enticements draw them. Rather than returning to their first love, they turn to someone else. Innocent at first, the attraction becomes more than a flirtation. The kindling turns to a flame. Sam and Denise? Their passion gets left on the altar of their wedding vows, a pile of cold ashes. They have, in effect, backslidden in their marriage as the perverse spirit slithered in and out, wreaking havoc once again.

Unfortunately, a Christian can fall into the same traps regarding his relationship with Jesus. When Greg* first comes to the Lord, his love is fresh, exciting, and exhilarating. Jesus means everything to him, and they share sweet fellowship.

As time goes by, the busyness of, dare I say, "ministry" gets in the way. Soon, "ministry" needs this, and "ministry" needs that. The pressures of "ministry" overwhelm Greg, drain his vitality, and draw him away from the Lover of his every breath. Weariness of mind and body compete with his devotion to the Lord. Meanwhile, the perverse spirit subtly slips in and out, bringing one hindrance after another, all under the guise of "ministry."

Influences outside the church tug at his soul. He slips into complacency in his relationship with God while slipping into worldly pursuits that appeal to his senses. Seemingly innocent, they eventually lead to devastating results. The passion for Jesus becomes a memory. Greg wakes one morning, goes about his day, with no thought of the One who gave up all for him. Haunting verses of worship songs he once sang with exuberance echo faintly in the back of his mind. Unaware of the deception he slipped into, he is now another life turned quite around—a sad portrayal of a soul once full of zeal for the Lord.

The question now? Do hindrances keep you too busy to spend time with the Lord? Do you play with the world because your passion for God resembles a dying ember? How far have you slipped? Bow in humble adoration and lift up this prayer with me to our Beloved Lord:

God, I come to you in fear and trembling. You are holy and awesome, and I have nothing to offer you except my backslidden ways. I neglected you and allowed other things to fill my heart. I deceived myself into thinking I didn't need anyone. I turned away from you and followed what felt good and looked good, all to serve my own purposes. Oh God, I am cold and empty inside. Please have mercy on me. Forgive me and deliver me from this perverse spirit.

Holy Spirit, burn the dross out of me and stir up a holy zeal inside. I renew my betrothal to you, Jesus, my Bridegroom. Seal your love upon me. Let me never again turn from you. You are my all, my everything. I worship you, my God and King, in Jesus' name. Amen.

Now do the prayer. Worship Him. Spend time with the One who set you as a seal on His heart and engraved your image on the palms of His hands. He's worth your all.

A Crooked Little Man Walked a Crooked Little Mile

Funny how an old nursery rhyme can help us find hidden riches in dark places.[43] An aspect of *backsliding* comes from the perspective of a Christian who accepts Jesus as Lord and Savior but continually turns back to his old way of life. He wears a path to the altar, repeatedly renewing his commitment to God. Truly repentant, he senses the presence of the Lord. Yet within a short time, he's living for the world, the devil, or himself.

A Hebrew word translated in Scripture as crooked supports the idea of the habitual backslider. It means to *seize by the heel, to circumvent as if by tripping up the heels, to restrain as if holding by the heel, and to take by the heel.*[44]

Moreover, Psalm 49:5 plainly describes this tactic of the enemy, ". . . the *iniquity* at my heels surrounds me." By applying this definition to our backslidden Christian, a distinct picture emerges. A perverse spirit seizes his heel to hinder him from making progress in his walk with the Lord, trips his heel to keep him from walking the path God called him to, or holds his heel to prevent him from getting established in his faith in God.

In Mark 4, Jesus talked about this type of believer in the parable of the sower:

Some [seed] fell on stony ground, where it did not have much earth; and immediately it sprang up because it had no depth of earth. But when the sun was up it was scorched, and because it had no root it withered away. . .

These likewise are the ones sown on stony ground who, when they hear the word, immediately receive it with gladness; and they have no root in themselves, and so endure only for a time. Afterward, when tribulation or persecution arises for the word's sake, immediately they stumble. (Mark 4:5–6, 16–17)

Invariably, this scenario plays out again and again for people like Andrew.* He hears the Word of God. Though full of exuberance for the Lord, his life remains his own. He does his own thing, goes his own way. While glad for salvation, he makes no effort to grow in Christ.

Having no roots, when trouble comes to trip him up—and it will surely come—Andrew easily falls away. After months of being miserable, he hears the Word of God again. He walks down the aisle again. He gets excited again. But still does his own thing, goes his own way. When trouble, aka perverse spirit, grabs hold of him—and it will surely grab hold—Andrew falls away again.

In the Old Testament, the book of Judges reveals a similar pattern. The Israelites serve God, go their own way, fall into bondage, cry out to God; God sends a judge to deliver them. Then they serve God, go their own way, fall into bondage, cry out to God; God sends a judge to deliver them, and the pattern repeats. Looking back, their bad choices led them down this trail. The culprit behind those choices? I believe the perverse spirit pointed the way.

Whatever methods the sly serpent employs, he tailor-makes them for the victim like a Saks Fifth Avenue suit. Trouble at work or home. The lure from friends to join worldly pursuits. Unconfessed sin or a serious addiction. Whatever the problem, this archenemy takes advantage of any weakness to accomplish his plan, which is, of course, to steal, kill, and destroy.

Are you one of his victims? Does the path to the altar show the outline of your shoes? Do you keep getting tripped up? Have you backslidden for the umpteenth time? If yes, remember our only defense is the Lord of Hosts and His Word, which says, "My grace is sufficient for you, for My strength is made perfect in weakness" (2 Cor. 12:9). Thank God for His grace! And thank God each of us can come before Him and pray with humble hearts:

Thank you, Lord, for your unfailing love and mercy. Arms open wide, you run to embrace me. Forgive my backsliding heart. Wash me with the precious blood of Jesus and purge me from my hidden faults. Lead me in paths of righteousness for your name's sake. Lord, set my feet on the Rock that is higher than me. Keep me from falling so I can walk before you in honor. Let your strength be perfected in my weaknesses. Baptize me again with your fire and power so I can walk in victory over the enemy.

In Jesus' name, I renounce my backslidden ways. I declare Jesus is my Lord and Savior. I choose to walk in righteousness before God. Holy Spirit, burn the chaff out of me and help me walk in purity and holiness. Give me a hunger for your Word to settle and establish me. I choose to turn from the vain and useless things of the world and run hard after you. I desire, above all, to be a shining star for you. I praise and bless you, Most Holy God, in Jesus' name. Amen.

Go ahead. Open your Bible to 1 John and spend time getting established in your faith. Expect Holy Spirit to meet you in the first verse. The two of you will have a splendid time of fellowship. Count on it!

Behind Prison Doors

Before we leave the section on backsliding, let's look at the criminal element and how it connects to the perverse spirit. Understanding the spiritual dynamics of this wily serpent provides a tool to set the captives free, in this case literally. Several Hebrew words demonstrate the link. A meaning for *crooked* actually means *fugitive,*[45] which comes from another term meaning *to bolt, to flee suddenly, to run away.*[46] One original root word for *perverse* means *fraud,*[47] and yet another one means *to do wickedly.*[48] All show the unmistakable correlation to crime. Various media outlets support this conclusion with daily news bulletins describing the horrific activities of criminals across the world. All too often the police put out APBs on armed and dangerous inmates who escape captivity.

On the other side of the more unsavory elements of criminal activity, white-collar crime impacts thousands, costing billions of dollars annually.[49] And don't ignore the high rate of teen runaways.[50] For many, this introduction to the shadier side of life leads them on a very crooked path. We need to look no further than biblical passages to confirm this. Proverbs warns of severe consequences for not seeking and following the wisdom of God. The second chapter provides a graphic illustration of this, "[**Without wisdom you will not be delivered**] from the way of evil, from the man who speaks *perverse* things, from those who leave the paths of uprightness to walk in the ways of darkness; who rejoice in doing evil and delight in the *perversity* of the wicked; whose ways are *crooked*, and who are devious in their paths . . ." (2:12–15). Quite a testimony for young people who ignore God's wisdom. Other verses demonstrate the fate of those who opt for a life of crime:

He who sows *iniquity* will reap sorrow. (Prov. 22:8)

The way of a guilty man is *perverse* . . . (Prov. 21:8)

He that hath a *froward* heart findeth no good: and he that hath a *perverse* tongue falleth into mischief. (Prov. 17:20 KJV)

A violent man entices his neighbor, and leads him in a way that is not good. He winks his eye to devise *perverse* things; he purses his lips and brings about evil. (Prov. 16:29–30)

As for such as turn aside to their *crooked* ways, the LORD shall lead them away with the workers of *iniquity*. (Ps. 125:5)

Their webs will not become garments, nor will they cover themselves with their works; their works are works of *iniquity*, and the act of violence is in their hands. Their feet run to evil, and they make haste to shed innocent blood; their thoughts are thoughts of *iniquity*; wasting and destruction are in their paths. The way of peace they have not known, and there is no justice in their ways; they have made themselves *crooked* paths; whoever takes that way shall not know peace. (Isa. 59:6–8)

None of these paint a picture of the good life!

Although time in jail should grant enough incentive to change, statistics show otherwise. Life in cages is not conducive to producing productive citizens. Crooked thinking begets crooked thinking. The recidivism rate of prison inmates may range upward to 70 percent.[51] Does *backsliding* ring a bell?

Statistics also show that most prisoners are male.[52] What better way to pervert the destiny of a nation! A perverse spirit turned loose in the lives of men who carry the seed for the next generation. Without the power of God and divine intervention, a vast number of criminals live out their days behind bars, outwitted by a master thief and robbed of their destiny.

Perhaps you know someone in prison. Or perhaps you live behind bars. Whatever the circumstance, know our infinite and wise God is well able to deliver you or your loved one. Nothing is too difficult. Nothing is impossible. We can boldly go before the throne of grace to pray:

God, we stand in the gap for those in prison and ask for a miracle. Invade their cells with your presence. Overshadow them with your glory. Pierce through the darkness on the inside of them. Deliver them from the bondages of the perverse spirit. Let them arise from their graves and shine like stars with the light of Christ. Send anointed men and women to minister your truth because your truth sets the captives free.

Lord Almighty, fill them with a passion for you. Let them become firebrands of glory and bring others to righteousness. As they put off the old man and become clothed with Christ, I ask for favor with the authorities over them. Make a way where there is no way. Prepare them for the freedom they will experience on the outside as they walk out the freedom they have on the inside. Bring others alongside to encourage them to press on. Let them run the race with their faces fixed on Jesus, the Author and Finisher of their faith. They are more than conquerors through Christ who loves them. Glory hallelujah! We bless and praise you, oh Most High God, in Jesus' name. Amen.

Don't quit. Don't give up. Keep pressing on. Keep persevering. Keep on keeping on because you win!

Dancing with Dragons

When did you last dance with a dragon? Last month? Last weekend? Two hours ago? Without realizing it, we dance with dragons every time we yield to pride. How does pride end up in a book about a perverse spirit, and what does dancing with dragons have to do with pride? A look at Scripture reveals the connection.

In the book of Job, God goes to great lengths to describe a leviathan, something we would call a dragon. He makes it abundantly clear that no man is able to stand against, let alone defeat, the leviathan. At the end of this discourse, found in Job 41, God declares the leviathan king of the children of pride.

Moving ahead to Isaiah 27, the first verse shows the link to the perverse spirit, "In that day the LORD with his sore [fierce] and great and strong sword shall punish leviathan the piercing serpent, even leviathan that *crooked* serpent; and he shall slay the dragon that is in the sea" (Isa. 27:1 KJV). Other translations use the following: c*oiling* (NIV); *twisted* (NASB); *coiling, writhing* (NLT); *wriggling, twisting* (TLB); and *twisting and winding* (AMP). Add a little music and unmistakable pictures of tantalizing dance moves fill the imagination.

Now run through your mind the various characteristics we have already uncovered. Any doubts how dancing with a dragon connects to pride, which then connects to the perverse spirit? The king of the children of pride is a crooked, coiling, twisted, writhing dragon, a perfect example of a perverse spirit working together with another principality.

Sadly, we don't have to look further than the church to see the two intertwine. Jesus dealt with them in His day, the Pharisees. Matthew 23 records His strong rebuke, "Woe to you, scribes and Pharisees, hypocrites! For you are like whitewashed tombs which indeed appear beautiful outwardly, but inside are full of dead men's bones and all uncleanness. Even so you also outwardly appear righteous to men, but inside you are full of hypocrisy and lawlessness [*iniquity*]" (vv. 27–28). A few verses later, Jesus called them "serpents" and a "brood of vipers."

Can you see the correlation? Today we don't have Pharisees. We just have pews full of religious people who walk in more pride than most unbelievers. Same spirit, different name. Smug in their religious suits, this brand of Christianity gets comfortable with a perverse spirit mingling in their midst.

At first, they seem sincere in their faith, pursuing purity and holiness with fervent zeal. Before long, chinks appear in their outward righteousness. They take on "ownership" of the church building. They turn arrogant and mean-spirited, their words cruel and vicious. They distort the truth to fit their agenda. Meddlesome busybodies, they actively pursue perverse disputings. Their demands on other Christians cause these poor souls to try to earn their way to heaven. Too holy to be touched by sinners, their distorted view of God drives the lost away from their only salvation.

Let me introduce you to Claude.* When you first meet him, Claude appears sincere. He spends hours praying in the church and prayer-walking in the city. He pursues holiness and wants the church in her rightful place as the bride of Christ. He desires to see the glory of God manifest in the house of the Lord. He loves to worship with banners. He makes sure his family attends church every Sunday. Outwardly, he appears to be an upstanding Christian.

Unfortunately, Claude's life presents a perfect example of these two crooked serpents. In reality, he spends so much time praying at the church and elsewhere, he has no time for his family. He places unreasonable demands on his wife and children in an attempt to satisfy his illogical mandates. Angry much of the time, his words are cruel. He uses God to fit his agenda. He then blames God when prayers aren't answered according to his expectations. At work, he disdains the "heathen" sitting next to him. He deems them too unclean and worldly to pray for. Besides, he's not called to pray for souls; his calling is for the house of the Lord.

And yet, this man doesn't care if a church building, including the one he attends, turns into a parking lot or a gas station. He only wants people to recognize the glory and presence of God on him when he walks into a room. His worship with banners is a frenzied activity of whipping the flags back and forth as he hurries up and down the aisle. All of this in the name of Jesus and for the glory of God.

What a tragic commentary! Instead of crowned with God's glory and honor, the leviathan crowns him with pride and arrogance. Instead of following the way, the truth, and the life, he pursues a twisted and tortuous path led by the perverse spirit. Unfortunately, he does not stand alone. Although the outward manifestations may differ, this demonic duo deceives numerous Christians into dancing with dragons. They sincerely believe they're serving God, but in reality, their masters are leviathan, the king of the children of pride, and the perverse spirit, the granddaddy of them all.

Before we stop the music, a little further investigation will demonstrate how drunkenness adds to the mix:

Woe to the crown of *pride*, to the drunkards of Ephraim. (Isa. 28:1)

Do not look on the wine when it is red, when it sparkles in the cup, when it swirls around smoothly; at the last it bites like a *serpent*, and stings like a *viper*. Your eyes will see strange things, and your heart will utter *perverse* things. (Prov. 23:31–33)

. . . It is not for kings to drink wine, nor for princes intoxicating drink; lest they drink and forget the law, and *pervert* the justice of all the afflicted. (Prov. 31:4b, 5)

If you stand in close proximity to someone who over-imbibes, this is no new revelation. Drunken people strut around full of arrogance before they stumble and fall because they can't stand up straight. Their words turn around faster than the sun disappearing at the North Pole in December. Unless drinking mellows them out, they exhibit cruel, vicious, and abusive behavior. Their perception of life gets twisted. While under the influence, they no longer distinguish truth from fantasy.

Married to a man who abused alcohol, walked in pride, and lived in bondage to a perverse spirit, at one point, my life showcased the destruction these three strongholds can inflict on a family. Together, they leave paths of catastrophic devastation, shipwrecking the destinies of multitudes again and again and again.

So back to the original question: When did you last dance with a dragon? If you sense conviction in your heart, you may be reliving some moments when the two of you shared a waltz or maybe a little tango. Thank God we can come boldly to His throne of grace and ask Him to slay the crooked serpent:

Father God, we stand before your majesty with broken and contrite hearts. Our sin of pride has left us weighing in the balance. Our righteousness is nothing but filthy rags in your presence. Our holier-than-thou, self-righteous prayers bring a stench before your throne. Compared to the pure light emanating from your Spirit, our lives are dark caverns full of vain and useless idols. We deserve nothing less than every judgment meted out alongside the wicked.

Lord, we ask forgiveness for causing others to turn from you because of the arrogance we displayed. Jesus, draw each one back to you. Heal their wounded souls. Touch their hearts with your healing balm and restore them to wholeness.

Almighty God, take your two-edged sword and slay this twisted, crooked serpent. Deliver us from the judgment we deserve. Let your mercies rain down on us every morning. With humility for our inner garments, help us to live out your Word and do justly, love mercy, and walk humbly before you. Eternal God, we place you on the highest place to rule in our hearts. Hallelujah to the Lamb who was slain! Thank you for your unfailing love and mercy, in Jesus' name . . .

Take more time to worship Jesus. Get on your knees, get on your face, bow your heart and worship Him in spirit and in truth. When you finish, if you ever do, you put the Amen on this prayer.

Let's Play Hide 'n' Seek

The last treasure of darkness. Wow! All I can say is thank God! I don't know about you, but at times I wondered if this chapter had an ending. Thankfully, the relentlessness of God and the encouragement of my intercessors did not allow me an escape hatch. Now for a look at this final nugget, this hidden gem.

While writing about the tummy troubles, the Lord reminded me of another incident I experienced after completing the study. It uncovered one more sinister characteristic. At the time, a perverse spirit was not only *not* in the ballpark, he couldn't be found in the parking lot! Yet, the wily serpent used this manifestation to remain under wraps and unhindered. Consequently, he continued twisting crooked paths for unsuspecting victims.

What brought this concealed trait to light? Flu symptoms. I woke up one morning with a headache and slight nausea. Although I spoke healing verses over myself, the headache got worse and my nausea increased. Still, as mothers do, I carried on.

After lunch, I spread out a special blanket we used for family prayer time. I gathered my girls and, once we were settled, began praying in tongues. Immediately, a perverted sexual image popped into my head. Rather shocked, I quickly rebuked it. A few minutes later, another one danced across my mind. I cast it down too. When the third one hit, I got mad. I thought *You ugly sucker!* I bound up a perverse spirit, broke his assignment over me, and commanded him to go to the footstool of Jesus, all in the name of Jesus.

Immediately, every flu symptom left. Trying to wrap my head around what had just happened left me flabbergasted! What I mistakenly assumed was the flu, and rightfully so, turned out to be the perverse spirit *looking* like the flu. Deciding to do a little research, I went to the closet, opened *that* drawer, pulled out *that* file, and discovered a buried treasure. One of the meanings for *perverse* includes the idea of *disguising*,[53] which is exactly what the wily serpent did; he disguised himself as the flu.

My response? Total shock, almost to the point of denial. How had I missed this aspect of the slippery snake? I stared at the word, my thoughts churning. *This can't be right. A perverse spirit doesn't cause flu symptoms.* Nothing in my grid had space for this new revelation. But the jolt to my organized word study did not alter the definition from Strong's.

Memories flooded my mind, images of ugly scenes scurrying across my imagination. Realizing how the perverse spirit had covertly damaged and destroyed so much of my life on so many levels left me speechless, numb with shock. Days passed as I struggled to come to grips with my new understanding. Eventually, with God's help, I moved on. Still, this aspect of the perverse spirit impacted me more than anything I had discovered on my journey.

Perhaps this has left you reeling with devastation from your own grief of things lost. As much as I want to close this chapter, I feel the heart of God wanting to minister to you. Let's pray:

Abba Father, you are the God of all comfort. I ask you to soothe the hearts and minds of those reliving the trauma of agonizing memories. Let your blanket of peace cover them. Hide them under your wing and give them rest for their troubled souls. Jesus, please repair their shattered lives. Pour out your marvelous grace and endless mercy until they rise again with joy in their hearts and songs of praise on their lips, in your precious name. Amen.

Don't rush through this healing process. Spend time with the One who created time and let Him bind up your wounded heart. You'll be glad you did.

In light of this revelation, a question bears asking: Can we even count the number of times we confronted a stronghold of anger, lying, or jealousy, to name a few, when we needed to deal with a perverse spirit? Highly unlikely. Because I believe him to be the "granddaddy" of all evil spirits, he is, in effect, the "king of the hill" in demonic hierarchy. However, if another one takes the brunt of the warfare, in my case a spirit of infirmity, the shifty serpent remains undiscovered and continues twisting the plans and purposes of God. This characteristic has allowed him to remain incognito throughout the millennia—until he tempted me with ungodly, immoral thoughts, overplaying his hand, numbering his days.

At this point, you may wonder whether the perverse spirit sabotages everything. The answer? Maybe, sort of, kind of, probably, well, I guess. Before I explain, let me share a few incidents that happened to a couple of my friends. Many years ago, Teresa called and asked me to pray for her daughter, who was exhibiting extreme jealousy toward her siblings. Despite many prayers, Teresa had seen no shift. Holy Spirit prompted me to encourage her to deal with the perverse spirit. Sure enough, her daughter's attitude changed, and the family experienced a breakthrough.

A number of years ago, Heidi and I met for fellowship and prayer. She didn't feel well due to flu symptoms. She had prayed and taken various natural health remedies, but saw no improvement. I suggested we come against the perverse spirit. The result? Symptom free in minutes.

Not long ago, Heidi called for prayer. As a CNA (Certified Nursing Assistant), she needed full capacity in her hands to take care of residents in a local nursing home. Yet, this day, for no apparent reason, her thumb had swollen to nearly double in size, along with severe shooting pains. We prayed over the phone, and by the time we finished, she had some relief. However, I did not pray regarding the perverse spirit.

Later in the day, I stopped by her house after doing errands. She showed me her thumb and commented about feeling something twisted on the inside. Upon hearing this, I took her hand, prayed again, and specifically dealt with the perverse spirit. Before she went to work, her thumb was its normal size and pain-free. She had no issues performing her duties on the night shift nor has she suffered from this malady since.

Now back to my very original answer: Maybe, sort of, kind of, probably, well, I guess. This was Rebekah's standard response when she didn't want to answer "yes" to one of my questions. At this point, I really don't want to have to say yes because that would mean the perverse spirit probably is behind everything, and I don't even want to go there. But the answer? Maybe, sort of, kind of, probably, well, I guess. Keep in mind, he's the "granddaddy" of them all. The biggest, nastiest, ugliest sucker to exist! (I haven't yet explained how, but stay with me. We'll get there.) His purpose? To twist, distort, stretch, make crooked, and turn upside down the destiny of every person with the breath of life.

With this newfound revelation, you may wonder how to know which spirit you're up against. I suggest you deal with the one manifesting the symptoms. If you see no improvement or breakthrough, then go after the perverse spirit.

Regardless of what we do, or even the outcome, we are more than conquerors through Jesus. In spite of how it looks, in spite of how much baggage we carry, in spite of how often we fall, God always causes us to triumph in Christ Jesus. Check out Romans 8:37 and 1 Corinthians 15:57. Even though Paul wrote them almost two thousand years ago, the messages still carry invaluable truths today. We win! Hallelujah! Glory to God! Let's worship Him together!

Lord Most High, you are brilliant! Thank you for all these incredible hidden treasures and secret riches! Your truth brings us freedom in ways we never thought possible. Who would have thought three nails could deliver us? Who would have dreamed a tree could be the instrument to break curses? Who would have imagined a whip could bring healing to broken spirits and sick bodies? Only you could bring forth this master plan to set us free.

We honor you, Jesus, for willingly and joyfully suffering for us. How does someone say thank you to the only One who could save us not just from hell, but from a life of hell? We love you, precious Savior. We are yours and yours alone. Holy Spirit, thank you a million times over for bestowing on us our heavenly rewards. We love and adore you. Glory, glory, glory to our Great and Mighty God!

What an incredible journey! Take time in His presence to bask in His wonderful goodness, His profound grace, His unchanging love. He's looking forward to being with you. You are, after all, His favorite.

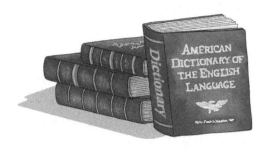

CHAPTER 3

Thank God for Noah Webster!

Noah Webster? How does the guy who wrote the dictionary fit into this? My mind is still reeling from everything you've written just from Strong's and the Bible! I fully admit I had no idea, not a clue. This perverse spirit devil is everywhere. I can see him all over the place and in everything, including me. OUCH!

But how did he get started in the first place? He didn't just show up one day. He had to come from somewhere. You said he's the "granddaddy" of all the demonic spirits, but I thought pride got Lucifer kicked out of heaven. That's what I've heard in sermons, anyway. How can the perverse spirit be the head honcho?

Good questions. I asked the same ones, with no answers. For a long time, I didn't see the connection. I discussed it with Teresa, and we concluded the perverse spirit had to be in the garden with Adam and Eve. Unfortunately, I didn't have Scripture to back it up. Every once in a while I pondered it, but the dots were all over the page with no starting point.

A few years went by. One day while reading in Genesis, I came to chapter 15 where God cut a covenant with Abraham. He talked about the bondage Abraham's descendants would suffer in a land not their own. The Lord said He would deliver them after four hundred years, but not until the Amorites fulfilled their *iniquity*. Curious about a massive tool with the ability to keep an entire nation in bondage for hundreds of years, I grabbed Strong's. Completely astonished, I discovered it came from the same Hebrew root as *perverse*, number #5766, meaning *(moral) evil: iniquity, perverseness, unjust (-ly), unrighteousness (-ly), wicked (-ness)*.[54]

Suddenly, a line connected between two dots, then another, and another. Remembering a teaching from Ezekiel 28 describing Lucifer's exit from heaven, I reached for my Bible and, to my amazement, discovered the perverse spirit in the garden of Eden.

To answer your questions, let's review the first page of Chapter One and ". . . the days of perfection in heaven. Days of matchless beauty, awesome majesty, perfect . . . until the day . . . What day? The day sin found a place in heaven, through Lucifer." Ezekiel portrayed it like this:

> You were the seal of perfection, full of wisdom and perfect in beauty.
> You were in Eden, the garden of God;
> every precious stone was your covering;
> the sardius, topaz, and diamond, beryl, onyx and jasper,
> sapphire, turquoise, and emerald with gold.
> The workmanship of your timbrels and pipes
> was prepared for you on the day you were created.
> You were the anointed cherub who covers; I established you;
> you were on the holy mountain of God;
> you walked back and forth in the midst of fiery stones.
> You were perfect in your ways from the day you were created,
> till *iniquity* was found in you. (Ezek. 28:12b–15)

Most, if not all preachers, use this passage to expound on the sin of pride—Lucifer radiated perfection in all his ways until pride led to his demise. As we saw earlier, Isaiah 14 painted a vivid description of the arrogance in his heart.

However, Ezekiel doesn't mention pride until verse 17, which is **after** *iniquity* was found in him. Why no one noticed this or preached on it is one of those questions with a million dollar answer. Looking back at the above Scripture, we see Lucifer, the seal of perfection: Covered with precious stones. Created with musical instruments. Carried the anointing of God. Established on God's holy mountain. Granted a place in the garden of Eden. Perfect. No flaws, no scars, no blemishes, no defects. Perfect. Until *iniquity*, or rather *perverseness*, was found in him. What a horrible, horrible tragedy! **Perverted perfection became perfected evil** and slithered into the place he called home, deceiving the created likeness of God on the earth.

How did it happen? This is where Noah Webster comes into play. God ordained him from before the foundations of the world to pen the first American dictionary. Today, strong references to his Christian faith can be found in the definitions. Throughout the twenty-seven years it took him to complete his work, God dropped heavenly insights into his spirit. Again, I say, thank God for Noah Webster.

If you recall, when I wanted to learn more about a word, I checked out Strong's and followed up with Webster's. I always found amazing revelations in the dictionary. This study followed the same pattern. Once I exhausted the concordance, I opened up the dictionary to find confirmations regarding the characteristics of the perverse spirit. Rather than narrowing the focus, Webster's gave breadth and depth to what I had already uncovered.

And this led me to understand exactly how the perverse spirit made his moves in the garden of Eden. One of the synonyms Webster included is *vitiate* which means *to make faulty or defective often by the addition of something that impairs*. The word so intrigued me, I never forgot it. Several years later the dots connected, and the perverse spirit rose up before my eyes. If you pay close attention, you might figure it out yourself.

Let's join Adam and Eve in the garden when the serpent worked his wiles and replay the conversation that fateful day:

And [the serpent] said to the woman, "Has God indeed said, 'You shall not eat of every tree of the garden'?" And the woman said to the serpent, "We may eat the fruit of the trees of the garden; but of the fruit of the tree which is in the midst of the garden, God has said, 'You shall not eat it, nor shall you touch it, lest you die.'"

Then the serpent said to the woman, "You will not surely die. For God knows that in the day you eat of it your eyes will be opened, and you will be like God, knowing good and evil." (Gen. 3:1b–5)

Do you see what Eve did? Notice the last part of her response. Now compare hers to what God actually said in Genesis 2:16–17:

And the LORD God commanded the man, saying, "Of every tree of the garden you may freely eat; but of the tree of the knowledge of good and evil you shall not eat, for in the day that you eat of it you shall surely die."

God never said Adam couldn't *touch* the tree. God only said Adam couldn't *eat* of the tree. Because of the influence of the perverse spirit, Eve **added** to the Word of the Lord, which **impaired** the Word of the Lord, and then **perverted** the plans and purposes of God for Adam and Eve. The addition to God's clear Word resulted in Eve's deception and Adam's open rebellion. In the garden, God's home away from home, perverted truth took the place of pure truth. The perverse spirit began his tortuous path through the millennia to make crooked places for all made in the likeness of God.

Although *vitiate* turned out to be a gold mine, Webster's contained many priceless nuggets. The following is a partial list of definitions and synonyms for *perverse, untoward, froward, crooked, and iniquity*:

1. Contrary to the evidence or the direction of the judge on a point of law
2. Obstinate in opposing what is right or reasonable (wrongheaded)
3. Arising from or indicative of stubbornness or obstinacy
4. Marked by peevishness
5. Misdirect, misuse, misinterpret
6. To cause to turn aside or away from what is good or true or morally right
7. To cause to become lowered or impaired in quality or character
8. Habitually disposed to disobedience and opposition
9. Contrary

10. To make disloyal
11. Invalidate
12. Temperamentally unwilling to accept advice
13. Restive (stubbornly resisting control; fidgety; restless)
14. Balky (refusing to proceed)
15. Unwilling or unable to conform to custom or submit to authority
16. Deviating from rectitude (righteousness; moral integrity; straight)
17. Oblique (underhanded)
18. Difficult to guide, manage, or work with
19. Marked by trouble or unhappiness
20. Gross injustice

Quite an impressive list, don't you think? Someone's top twenty countdown, perhaps? In all seriousness, we see *perverseness* leads to rebellion rather than obedience and exalts the foolishness of man over the wisdom of God. And surprise, surprise, numerous Scriptures back up Noah's own insights:

A worthless person, a wicked man, walks with a *perverse* mouth . . . (Prov. 6:12)

But the *perverseness* of transgressors shall destroy them. (Prov. 11:3b KJV)

. . . he who is *perverse* in his ways despises [the Lord]. (Prov. 14:2b)

Better is the poor who walks in his integrity than one who is *perverse* in his lips, and is a fool. (Prov. 19:1)

The foolishness of a man twists [*perverts*] his way, and his heart frets against the Lord. (Prov. 19:3)

Better is the poor who walks in his integrity than one *perverse* in his ways, though he be rich. (Prov. 28:6)

> Whoever walks blamelessly will be saved, but he who is *perverse* in his ways will suddenly fall. (Prov. 28:18)

Proverbs makes it clear that God's blessing follows those who walk in integrity, including financial prosperity. The path of the perverse, however, leads to destruction. No amount of money can save him.

My excitement when I connected the final dot didn't hit the moon; it flew past Jupiter! I called Teresa, and we both rejoiced, thanking God for Noah Webster. Between Scriptures written under divine inspiration by God, and the dictionary, written by a fiercely committed believer, Holy Spirit led me to write *Making Crooked Places Straight*. Obviously, Noah and I don't compare to the Holy Scriptures; nonetheless, neither of us would have been able to complete the work set before us without the divine influence of heaven upon our hearts and the outward manifestation of it in our lives. That, by the way, is a paraphrase of the Greek definition for *grace*.[55] Wow! Isn't that amazing?

CHAPTER 4

And Behind Door # . . .

Doors? What is this, Let's Make a Deal? *I'm not opening the door to a perverse spirit. And I'm not making any deals with him either . . . Wait a minute, just how many doors are there? What if I've already opened some? How do I close them? And besides, shouldn't churches do something about them? Except, I haven't heard this in all the sermons I've listened to. Help!*

Opening a door. What a simple task. And yet, when a door opens for the perverse spirit, trouble with a capital T waltzes in. Soon walking becomes difficult. Stumbling blocks abound on the twisted path, courtesy of the cunning serpent. Early on, destiny appears within easy reach. Down the road? Not so much.

Although any sin, whether of omission or commission, opens the door to the enemy, the perverse spirit uses two specific means to walk in and take up residence in our lives. Door #1 is rebellion, as we saw in the last chapter. Granted, we may not perceive it immediately. Other times, we flat out choose defiance. Either option steers a believer down a crooked road. Full of hairpin turns, this path leads to derailed destinies. Still, if you follow God for any length of time and delight yourself in Him, obedience becomes your sustenance. You find yourself eating the good of the land, just as Isaiah prophesied (1:19).

Should you notice rebellion in an area of your life, you know what to do: **REPENT!** Seriously, get with it. Ask for forgiveness, and then repent. Change the way you think. Return to the highest point of your relationship with God. Do what you need to in order to shut that door. If you don't know, fast and pray to get the mind of Christ. Then do it. Obedience. This not only shuts the door, repentance fastens a dead bolt lock on it. If you sense the conviction of Holy Spirit, do it now. Don't wait. Your future, your destiny, your very life are at stake.

Now for door #2. Can anything entice you to open this door? Perhaps

a description of the contents may tempt you to look through the peephole. How about spurned and discarded? Jilted and cast off? Brushed aside and a cold shoulder? Ostracized and unwelcome? Scorned and abandoned? Any clues yet? If you opened your front door and saw any one of those packages waiting to be delivered, you wouldn't touch it. Yet, we believers open it most frequently to the perverse spirit.

What exactly waits behind door #2? Rejection! While coming in different shapes and sizes, with a variety of signatures, no one willingly holds out the welcome mat for it. No one wants to feel the sting of rejection. It's tormenting, debilitating, crippling, paralyzing, and a host of other afflictions.

Case in point, divorces. Millions of people, young and old, adults and children, walk across this land carrying wounds of rejection because of divorce.[56] Beginning with words spoken in anger and ending with words written in a divorce decree, the perverse spirit has a heyday distorting the purposes of God for these families as the pain of rejection pierces deep.

If you remember, Chapter Two includes several sections covering the power of words and what occurs when this wicked entity is the moving force behind them. A verse in the section on "Cruel and Unusual Words of Punishment" bears repeating, "A wholesome tongue is a tree of life, but *perverseness* therein is a breach in the spirit" (Proverbs 15:4 KJV). For a quick refresher, *breach* comes from Hebrew with the idea of *fracture*.[57] Other meanings include *bruise, crushing, destruction, and hurt*.

Imagine Janet* and Dave receive these words and actions from each other. Without proper handling of the wounds, the perverse spirit smears his images on their fractured hearts and minds. Distorted perspectives of each other and a skewed view of God paint tragic consequences on the landscape of their marriage. Janet slips into a depression, Dave finds solace in a bottle, and two broken hearts bleed on the inside. Sound familiar?

Furthermore, divorce isn't the only leader of the pack when it comes to rejection. How many receive pink slips at work? Or get fired, like me? With the shaking of world economies in these last days, a common scenario plays out in one company after another. This is due, in part, to a rebellious bent against God and His spiritual laws that some top CEOs pursue. Do I hear crackling sounds as the serpent slithers amongst the hundred-dollar bills spilling out of pockets as they pay the piper for the dance? Unfortunately, these CEOs force employees, through no fault of their own, to pay the piper via job losses. This form of rejection carries its own brand of pain, embarrassment, and humiliation.

And trust me, the perverse spirit will make sure you have a warped image of the face you see in the mirror. But warped images don't get left on the bathroom mirror. They walk out the front door every morning and carry rejection with them. Because it's a common visitor, every day, every hour, every minute rejection knocks on someone's door. We find the most bruising and destructive ones in our closest relationships: Husbands and wives, parents and children, teachers and students, childhood friends. Each can fracture because of rejection. When they do, more crooked places etch into their souls.

What about rejection within the Christian community? Scores of people leave churches because of it. This rejection can come from a number of different sources. A wrong look from the pastor sends people out the door. Judgmental attitudes lead others to look elsewhere. The "my way or the highway" mentality from leadership propels Christians to seek the exits.

Unfortunately, deep rejection also causes believers to use their gifts and callings to gain acceptance in the body of Christ. As a result, the believer gets lifted up instead of God. Since these gifts and callings don't come forth in a clean and pure ministry unto the Lord, the perverse spirit does what he does best—makes crooked places in their lives.

Furthermore, many Christians assume acceptance in the body of Christ depends on church leadership welcoming their giftings. When they don't receive the recognition they desire, rejection, via the perverse spirit, whispers, "You deserve better than this. You can find another church that will really appreciate you." These words echo in their minds while they march out one door and into another, desperately seeking approval and appreciation. These believers walk a tortuous path for years without understanding the biblical truth written in Ephesians 1:6—Abba Father already accepted them in the beloved.

Before we shut door #2 and throw away its key, let's bring this a little closer to home. My home. Remember the story about Rebekah's tummy troubles. Some of you may have wondered at the time how or why a perverse spirit could attack an innocent little baby. You may have questioned too why Rebekah suffered and not Holly.

To answer the second question, he did attack both of their digestive systems. Although I had an easy pregnancy with Holly, her first few weeks caused stress for all of us. She couldn't keep anything down, and blood spotted her stools. She continued losing weight, even though she nursed an hour and a half almost every three hours when awake. My desperation neared a breaking point as I continually cried out to God.

When she was a month old, we went to a prophetic conference. The speaker prayed over her, and God gave him a word of knowledge concerning her digestive tract. Completely healed, we all rejoiced over the Lord's compassion.

For the first question, the "why" part is clear. The perverse spirit wants to, plans to, and determines to steal, kill, and destroy. He doesn't care how he accomplishes his plan as long as he gets it done, and the sooner the better. Why do you think millions of babies, and counting, are killed in the womb?

The entire debate over the reproductive rights of a woman comes straight out of the perverse spirit's manual. Destroying babies is satan's primary goal from the day God cursed him to slither on the ground. Make no mistake, his relentless onslaught will continue until the final trumpet's sounds fill the air. My babies were not exempt from his handiwork.

To answer the "how" part is infinitely more difficult and grievous. With the realization that praying against the perverse spirit actually worked for Rebekah, I mulled over the study and concluded rejection was the culprit. A little background will provide some understanding. I love babies. From a young age, I wanted at least ten of my own. Seriously. After our marriage, my husband and I agreed to wait before starting a family.

Over the years, though, he became more reluctant to step into fatherhood. On the other hand, becoming a mother consumed me. Finally, after years of praying, weeping, and seeking the Lord, I became pregnant with our first child. My response? Complete over-the-top exuberance! After my first doctor appointment, I walked around the house, laughing and crying, praising God. My husband's response? Complete opposite. Angry and depressed, he pulled farther away from me and God. While Holly grew in my womb, rejection, along with the perverse spirit, laid the foundation to move against her tiny body as soon as she took her first breath.

When I found myself expecting two years later, my husband's response worsened. Furious words and cruel actions filled our house repeatedly. Eventually, he left me and my two babies, one not yet born. The perverse spirit, via rejection, began leaving his handiwork on Rebekah while I carried her. One night as I lay in bed, she stopped moving. At nearly eight months along, this little one bounced incessantly. Suddenly nothing. Just as quickly, thoughts of three people dying swam through my mind.

In a split second, I realized the devil intended to kill Rebekah by wrapping her umbilical cord around her neck. A righteous rage rose up on the inside. I went after the devil with everything I had.

"In Jesus' name, I command you, perverse spirit, to loose my baby and let her go. Unwrap her cord immediately! Death, I rebuke you! I speak life into my womb. No weapon formed against either of us will prosper. My child will live and not die."

I prayed in loud tongues, not caring who heard or who woke up. My baby's life mattered more than someone's interrupted sleep. Suddenly, a burst of flurry exploded on the inside of me. As the cord unwrapped, it felt as though someone took a roll of paper and let it fly.

In moments, I felt Rebekah moving. With peace in my heart and peace in my womb, I fell asleep. About one month later, she made her entrance, pink and healthy with no cord around her neck. Although he lost the battle in the womb, this wicked demon still came against her through her digestive tract.

I don't think the attacks against my babies were the exception to the norm. Many newborns experience some type of rejection in the womb or at birth. When they do, the perverse spirit stands by to twist their little tummies into knots, causing pain for the baby and anguish for the parents. As these little ones grow up, rejection continues to knock at the door. They can unwittingly open themselves to a very crooked path led by a crooked perverse spirit. How crooked? We live in the midst of a crooked and perverse generation. For proof, take a look at what's available on TV, the internet, or various social media sites.

Personally, I think it's time to lock the door to rejection and throw the key into the uttermost depths of the sea. How do we accomplish this? The Word of God, where all truth begins and ends in Jesus Christ, shows us the times Jesus Himself suffered rejection.

Rejected before He walked the earth:

He is despised and rejected by men, a Man of sorrows and acquainted with grief. And we hid, as it were, our faces from Him; He was despised and we did not esteem Him.

(Isa. 53:3. Note that Isaiah prophesied this 700 years before His birth.)

Rejected by His earthly father:

After His mother Mary was betrothed to Joseph, before they came together, she was found with child of the Holy Spirit. Then Joseph her husband, being a just man . . . was minded to put her away secretly. (Matt. 1:18–19)

Rejected by His family:
But when His own people heard about [the multitudes following Him], they went out to lay hold of Him, for they said, "He is out of His mind." (Mark 3:21)

Rejected by His followers:
Therefore many of His disciples, when they heard this, said, "This is a hard saying; who can understand it?" When Jesus knew in Himself that His disciples complained about this, He said to them, "Does this offend you? . . ." From that time many of His disciples went back and walked with Him no more. (John 6:60–61, 66)

Rejected by the church leaders:
So all those in the synagogue, when they heard [Jesus read Isaiah's prophecy], [they] were filled with wrath, and rose up and thrust Him out of the city . . . (Luke 4:28–29a)

Rejected by one of the twelve:
Then one of the twelve, called Judas Iscariot, went to the chief priests and said, "What are you willing to give me if I deliver Him to you?" (Matt. 26:14–15a)

Rejected by the rest of the twelve:
Then all the disciples forsook Him and fled. (Matt. 26:56b)

Rejected by one of His closest disciples:
Then [Peter] began to curse and swear, saying, "I do not know the Man!" (Matt. 26:74)

Rejected by His heavenly Father:
> And at the ninth hour Jesus cried out with a loud voice, saying . . .
> "My God, My God, why have You forsaken Me?" (Mark 15:34)

If anyone understands the pain of rejection, He's the One called Man of Sorrows. From before the womb until the tomb, He experienced rejection. How did Jesus handle it? He never opened the door to it. He fixed His eyes on the road leading to the cross and never wavered. He refused to allow anyone, and I mean anyone, to stop Him from fulfilling prophecy and His destiny, the cross. He stayed true to His Spirit, even while dying on the cross.

How, then, do we handle it? Run to the cross. Run to the cross. Run to the cross. Did I only say it three times? I'll say it again. Run to the cross. Run to the cross. Run to the cross. Jesus took rejection for us. All of it. He suffered rejection on every level. The writer of Hebrews tells us He became like us so He could identify with us:

> Since, therefore, [these His] children share in flesh and blood [in the physical nature of human beings], He [Himself] in a similar manner partook of the same [nature] . . . So it is evident that it was essential that He be made like His brethren in every respect . . . (Heb. 2:14, 17a AMP)

> Since the children are made of flesh and blood, it's logical that the Savior took on flesh and blood . . . It's obvious, of course, that he didn't go to all this trouble for angels. It was for people like us, children of Abraham. That's why he had to enter into every detail of human life. (Heb. 2:14, 17a MSG)

> Therefore, since the children share a common physical nature as human beings, he became like them and shared that same human nature . . .(Heb. 2:14, Jewish New Testament)

Not a single aspect of our lives escapes Jesus. He knows what makes us tick. He's walked a mile in our shoes. He gets us. According to 1 John 3:8, He came to earth to destroy the works of the perverse spirit. He meant it when he cried out on the cross, "It is finished!" We don't have to open the door to rejection. It's over. It really is finished.

Nonetheless, rejection still rings the doorbell. Our response when we hear the sound? Refuse the package! I will never forget the night I battled it out in my living room. The opportunity presented itself at work that day. As the receptionist of a national company, I shared an office with the three sales guys. Over the months we developed fun, teasing relationships. When the business moved to a new building, I had expected things to stay the same. Instead, with my desk in an isolated reception area, I seldom saw anyone, including the sales crew. The three almost completely ignored me; the camaraderie we once shared had vanished.

This particular morning, one of them turned especially nasty to me. Shocked and hurt, I called a friend for prayer. By the time I walked through my front door, rejection was trying to suffocate me. Sitting on the couch, I cried over and over, "I am not alone. I am not rejected. Jesus took my rejection on the cross." Tears ran down my face, but I kept on. "Your Word says I'm accepted in the Beloved. You promised to never leave me nor forsake me. Lord, help me to forgive him." For more than two hours the battle raged. Eventually, rejection lifted. I won that night because I pressed into God's truth until I had the victory.

A few weeks before this incident, I talked and prayed with another friend. I will never forget what he said. "Just remember this, Penelope. At the end of the day, when it's all said and done, you are not alone." While I had no inkling of the coming storm, God did, preparing the way for me. Today His truth reigns inside me—I am more than a conqueror through Christ. Nothing can separate me from the love of God in Christ Jesus. I am not alone. Not ever. Neither are you. Let's open our hearts to Him:

Oh God, we need you desperately. We are so fractured, Lord, so crushed. Pour the balm of Gilead upon our wounds. Let your healing virtue flow from your nail-scarred hands. Cover us with your precious blood. Father, we forgive every person who rejected us. Heal their wounded souls and repair their breaches. Bring them into wholeness. Draw them with cords of strong love into your family.

Lord, we repent for using our gifts to gain acceptance. Cleanse us and renew a right spirit within us. You are the Shepherd of our souls, and we cling to you. Walk into our yesterdays, close the doors to the places rejection came calling, and lead us in paths of righteousness for your name's sake.

God, remind us of who we are. Accepted in the Beloved. Given the spirit of adoption. Sealed upon your heart. Embraced with your unfailing love. All that we are, all that we have is in you. We open our hearts to the depth and height and length and width of your endless love. We worship and adore you, in Jesus' name. Amen.

What a holy God we have! Take time to rest in His love. Nothing else matters now.

Shall we proceed to door #3? This one takes us into the church, the community of believers. Surprisingly, Christians open this door on a frequent basis. Sometimes it's a wide chasm, other times only a sliver. Regardless of the size of the aperture, God steps back and permits the perverse spirit to slither right in and mingle with the crowd. What could possibly induce God to allow that to happen? Isaiah shows us how:

> The burden against Egypt. Behold, the LORD
> rides on a swift cloud, and will come into Egypt; the idols of Egypt
> will totter at His presence, and the heart of Egypt will melt in its
> midst. I will set Egyptians against Egyptians; everyone will fight

against his brother, and everyone against his neighbor, city against city, kingdom against kingdom. The spirit of Egypt will fail in its midst; I will destroy their counsel, and they will consult the idols and the charmers, the mediums and the sorcerers. And the Egyptians I will give into the hand of a cruel master, and a fierce king will rule over them . . .

The waters will fail from the sea, and the river will be wasted and dried up . . . The fisherman also will mourn . . . and those who weave fine fabric will be ashamed; and its foundations will be broken. All who make wages will be troubled of soul . . . The princes of Zoan have become fools; the princes of Noph are deceived; they have also deluded Egypt, those who are the mainstay of its tribes. *The Lord has mingled a perverse spirit in her midst*; and they have caused Egypt to err in all her work, as a drunken man staggers in his vomit. (Isa. 19:1–4a, 5, 8a, 9b–10, 13–14)

Although this prophecy judged Egypt because of her idolatry, 1 Corinthians 10:11 tells us everything written in the Old Testament is for our example. We also know from Galatians 4:22–31 that Egypt represents the flesh.

Move forward several millennia. The church today is not exempt from idolatry and the flesh. We consistently find prime examples throughout Christian gatherings. What do you think happens when we, the church, walk in idolatry or move in the flesh? We open door #3. The perverse spirit mingles in our midst and causes us to err. Since the section on "Funhouse Mirrors" in Chapter Two already describes how idolatry works hand in glove with the slippery serpent, this one will look at believers and their flesh. Let me share some scenarios demonstrating clear-cut choices:

Scenario #1

The worship leader, an anointed young man, seeks the Lord for the Sunday song list. He prepares well by praying and practicing with his team.

He feels confident, but not cocky. When he comes to the keyboard, he's ready for strong, rousing praise.

What the worship leader doesn't know? God just told a woman to leave her two children with family for five weeks while she attends an out-of-state school of ministry. She and her children have never been separated. Her family is antagonistic toward her because of her faith. She wants to obey the Lord, but she desperately needs to hear the loving voice of her heavenly Husband, her Maker, comforting her heart. She doesn't need hand-clapping, foot-stomping praise tunes. In fact, all morning she prayed, "Please, God, I can't handle loud praise today. I need quiet worship music. Please."

As the worship leader hits the chords for the first song, he senses Holy Spirit shifting into a gentler, more intimate style of worship. He now has a choice to make. Does he yield to his flesh and sing the up-beat songs from the list or does he follow the leading of Holy Spirit and sing the intimate songs?

Scenario #2

The pastor prepares for weeks, seeking the Lord's direction and vision for the church in the coming year. This Sunday morning he plans to present it to the people. During worship, the presence of God is palpable. At a critical moment, a woman breaks out in prophecy, the words electrifying. When she finishes, the pastor realizes a shift has taken place, and God has dropped a different message in his spirit. He now faces a decision. Does he yield to his flesh and share the vision for the coming year or does he follow the leading of Holy Spirit and preach the fresh manna from heaven?

Scenario #3

The evangelist finishes speaking. God's presence covers the room like a weighty blanket. Stillness presses on the people; expectations increase. Several minutes pass; the evangelist only looks at the crowd, smiling. A man feels the stirrings of tongues rising on the inside. A choice stands before him. Does he yield to his flesh and bring forth the message in tongues or does he follow the leading of Holy Spirit and stay quiet in the Lord's presence?

What happens if the worship leader, pastor, and evangelist choose obedience? God receives glory. People receive a blessing. What happens if they choose the flesh? Isaiah 19 goes into effect. To better understand the dynamics of what takes place when a perverse spirit actually *mingles*, Webster's definitions present a real eye-opener:

- *Mingle: To bring or mix together usually without any fundamental loss of identity*
- *Commingle: To blend thoroughly into a harmonious whole*
- *Blend: Combine in such a way so the line of demarcation can't be distinguished; to mingle intimately*
- *Merge: To blend gradually by stages that blur distinctions; to come together without abrupt change*
- *Coalesce: To grow together; unite into a whole*
- *Amalgamate: Merge into a single body*
- *Fuse: Make indissolubly one*

As the dictionary makes clear, this mingling produces an unholy mixture, resulting in a perversion of what God intended.

In Strong's, *err* has its own profound insights: *Vacillate, reel, go astray, seduce, stagger or wander.*[58] According to the dictionary, *vacillate* means to *waver in mind, will, and emotions; hesitate in choice of options, inability to take a stand.* Even more surprising, *vacillate* comes from a Latin word, *prevaricate,* meaning *to walk crookedly.*

Michael,* a leader in Sunday services, demonstrates this open door. During the service, he yields to his flesh instead of Holy Spirit. God grants permission for the perverse spirit to mingle. The congregation assumes all is well. The service continues. No one senses anything amiss. Due to the subtlety and deception, the people don't differentiate between the pure anointing or the mixture.

Look back at the previous scenarios. If those three individuals yielded to their flesh, most people in the pews would assume what was said or done came from the Lord, never knowing they received a defiled commingling. Regrettably, this process plays out repeatedly on church platforms.

If you attend more than a handful of Christian meetings, you probably experience people moving in their flesh. Obvious at times, others not so much. In the latter case, people think Holy Spirit is still moving, when in reality, a polluted mixture mingles amongst them, and according to Isaiah, causes them to err. Hopefully, once or twice doesn't derail someone's destiny. But regular occurrence in a group of believers ensures serious problems will ensue.

Unless someone recognizes the shift, the spirits of error and deception work in their hearts and minds, including the leadership. A once vibrant, living representation of Christ walks a crooked path to a destination crosswise to God's will and divine purpose.

The question: What do you do in a meeting when you become aware of someone moving in the flesh? Be willing to intercede and pray an identificational prayer of repentance to restore the pure anointing. Here is a prayer I have used:

Lord God, I come before you to stand in the gap on behalf of the leadership and the people in this meeting. We have sinned against you and you alone. We followed our own agendas and brushed aside yours. Forgive us for yielding to our flesh. Forgive us for not honoring your perfect plans above our own selfish goals. Holy Spirit, bring us back to the place we walked in before flesh began to lead.

In Jesus' name, I release the apostolic anointing, drawing every person into the highest place you have for them. I bind the perverse spirit from operating here, and I forbid him to manifest in any way. I once again lift up the name of Jesus and declare his Lordship over this meeting.

Almighty God, we choose to lay down our plans and look unto Jesus, the Author and Finisher of our faith. I declare that we all hear your voice and quickly obey. Holy Father, thank you for bringing everyone back to the high call of Christ in this gathering. I praise and bless you, in Jesus' name. Amen.

Does this work? Yes. The real keys in a prayer of this nature are threefold: A sincere heart of repentance in the one interceding, a release of the apostolic anointing, and a heart yielded to Holy Spirit. With this combination, the anointing flows again, the people revel in God's glories and grace, and the Lord Most High receives honor. Hallelujah!

Opened by Christians, door #4 results in immense heartache for everyone involved. Some churches never recover and close their doors. Many believers turn their backs on the church and God. Surprisingly, Scripture confirms this door. In Acts 20, Paul gathered the elders to encourage them as he bid farewell. We can pick it up in verse 28:

> Therefore take heed to yourselves and to all the flock, among which the Holy Spirit has made you overseers, to shepherd the church of God which He purchased with His own blood (v. 28).

> For I know this, that after my departure savage wolves will come in among you, not sparing the flock (v. 29).

> Also ***from among yourselves*** men will rise up, speaking ***perverse*** things, to draw away the disciples after themselves (v. 30).

What stands behind door #4? Splits. And I don't mean banana splits. I'm talking about church splits. Over the years, I've heard preachers expound on verses 28–29. Rarely does anyone preach on verse 30. To dissect this, we can use the time-honored method of the five Ws and How:

- Who: Men will rise up
- What: Speak perverse things
- When: After I leave
- Where: From among yourselves
- Why: To draw the disciples after themselves
- How: In a variety of ways

If you've never experienced a church split, then praise God. I mean that sincerely. You are, indeed, fortunate to have kept this door shut.

However, church splits occur more frequently than one would like. We see from Scripture the root is the perverse spirit. The original Greek gives the idea of *distortion and misinterpretation.*[59] Further study reveals a meaning *to twist, to turn quite around, or reverse.*[60] Do these definitions remind you of backsliding? Isn't this what happens to many believers after a church split? They become disillusioned with the leadership, then with the church, then with God. They turn quite around and head back out to the beckoning world.

How does a split happen? The worship leader thinks he's got the hottest voice; but he distorts his gift. The youth leader thinks he's got the biggest following; but he misinterprets his call. The intercessors think they have the only hotline to heaven in the church; but they twist God's intentions. The deacons think they have the inside track for the future of the church; but they misinterpret their purpose. The pastor thinks he has the greatest revelation next to Apostle Paul; but he distorts his ministry.

Remember the Lord's words before His last Passover in John 12:32, "And . . . if I be lifted up from the earth, [I] will *draw* all men unto me" (KJV). Notice Acts 20:30 and this verse both use *draw*. In one context, **Jesus** draws people to Himself; whereas, in the other one, **men** draw people to themselves. Regardless of the perpetrators, people distort, misinterpret or twist God's plans, turning others to follow after them instead of Jesus. As Christians, we need to be drawn to and seek after the Son of Man, Jesus, the Messiah. Anyone else, and a church split is around the corner.

Moreover, splits don't only happen in the church. Be it business partnerships, music groups, or families, splits have their roots in the perverse spirit. Someone speaks perverse things and draws others after themselves. This scenario happens repeatedly. Once good friends, former business partners pass each other on the street without speaking. Band members, who sang harmony together, file lawsuits against each other. Ugly divorces mar the once happy family portrait. Whether in the church or outside its walls, when this door opens, a split awaits at the threshold. God have mercy!

Time for a reality check. Did you answer the door when the perverse spirit came calling? Or did you get left behind while perverse words drew others away? In any case, let's pray:

Oh God in heaven, forgive us for opening doors to the perverse spirit, causing splits. We acted corruptly to achieve our own purposes. We took your name in vain to use for our own gain. We distorted truth to draw others after ourselves instead of pointing them to Jesus. We were more interested in our own puffed-up ideals than being yoked with the Savior and learning from Him. God, we are guilty as charged. We have no excuses. Our sin glares before us.

Forgive us and have mercy. Wash and cleanse us with the precious blood of Jesus. Bring us back into right relationship with you. Renew a right spirit within us. Repair every breach and bridge every schism.

Righteous God, we forgive those who wronged us, who led us astray by manipulating the truth. Set our feet once again on the Highway of Holiness as we follow hard after you. We also bring before you others affected by splits. Heal their wounded souls. Restore the joy of their salvation. Lead them on paths of righteousness back into the fold of the Shepherd of their souls. Make every crooked place straight in all of our lives. Let the banner of truth and righteousness wave once again over every church and home that they may be beacons of light, shining stars in the dark. Glory, glory, glory to our Most High King, in Jesus' name. Amen.

You may want alone time and an alone place with the Lord. Find a space and take the time—all the time you need.

Before we bring this chapter to a close, your last point needs to be addressed. Yes, the church needs to do something about the perverse spirit. Why aren't they? In the first place, you just read about two doors the church opens to welcome this wily serpent into her midst. It's a little hard to kick something out that you invite in. Second, do you remember the point you made at the beginning of Chapter One? Let me refresh your memory:

> *A perverse spirit? Who, me? In my church? How could you even think such a thing? Why, our church has the best worship this side of heaven! Our pastor preaches sermons so uplifting you would think God was standing in the pulpit. And as for me, I help in the church. I give over and above the tithe. I support other ministries, including two children in third-world countries. I read the Bible and pray, and not just before meals. I'm certainly not perfect, but a perverse spirit? Surely you jest! Of course, I know it's in the world. Why, the homosexual agenda is running rampant all over the place. Just take a look at what's on television, not to mention the big screen! And have you listened to some of the music out there? Talk about perverse! But not me, not my church. A perverse spirit? No way!*

In reality, your answer *is* the answer. For decades, the church assumed the perverse spirit only affected homosexuals or resulted from perverted sex. Because of the self-righteous, religious spirits much of the church walked in during those years, no one wanted to say anything connecting them to a perverse spirit. Consequently, the "see no evil, hear no evil, say no evil" mentality ruled in the midst of congregations. The slithering serpent continued to warp the plans and purposes of not only individuals, but entire churches.

During the process of putting the study together, I listened to preachers rebuke America for her sins. Each one described them with the same words found in Strong's or Webster's regarding *perverse*. Yet, not one of them said *perverse*. I don't think it was in their vocabulary. Nearly two years after I completed the study, God gave me a specific task dealing with the power of the perverse spirit over America.

The day after finishing it, I listened to another minister expound, again, on the moral failures of our country. Suddenly, out of his mouth came the word *perverse*. I did a double take and stood dumbfounded. For the first time, a preacher described events in our nation and the rest of the world as *perverse*. Soon others used it in their messages. Although they focused on the immoral aspects of perversion, it was a beginning. I shouted praises, dancing through my house!

Why don't you take time to do the same thing? After all, God has been breaking the power of the perverse spirit over your life throughout this book. If He's doing it in yours, He's doing it in the lives of others as well. Trust me, the day will come when the church, as a whole, will see the power of the perverse spirit broken within her walls. How do I know? God promised to make the crooked places straight and He can't lie. Hallelujah to the King!

CHAPTER 5

The Chicken Scratch Page and Other Insightful Tidbits

Didn't you mention chicken scratches somewhere in the beginning of the book? I was a little curious then. And tidbits? I hope they're bite-sized pieces because I don't think I can handle any more seven-course meals. But it does sound like it could make for interesting talk around the water cooler.

Chicken scratches around the water cooler. What an intriguing thought! As I realized the end of the book was just around the corner (Hooray! Yahoo! Glory! Hallelujah!), it occurred to me that you may have wondered about the chicken scratch page. After reviewing it, I noticed I had already discussed a few of the "scratches" but not all, hence, this chapter.

As you read through, you may think some belong in a previous section. Be that as it may, they were on the chicken scratch page, which I completely ignored while writing. I didn't want anyone to see it then, and I had no intention of including anything from it here. God obviously had other ideas. It appears Ilah heard from the Almighty when she kept sending out the page. I may not add all of them, but the ones I include will be somewhat informative and definitely enlightening.

The insightful tidbits come from notes I wanted to keep track of as I typed the manuscript. They didn't work in earlier chapters, but I felt they had enough value to add at some point. My plan? Briefly present the chicken scratch or insightful tidbit, give a little information, and leave you to ponder, meditate, dissect, and inspect. We'll see if my plan and God's plan line up and if these chicken scratches do indeed find themselves at the water cooler.

Chicken Scratch #1: Twisted thoughts.

Remember, according to Ezekiel 28, Lucifer was perfect in all his ways until *iniquity* (*perverseness*) was found in him. I believe when he took his eyes off Truth and focused on himself, his thoughts twisted. At that moment, he pulled the heavenly worship from God to himself and drew one-third of the angels after him. Since then, they have left twisted trails behind them wherever they go. The same thing happens to us when we take our eyes off Truth, Jesus Christ, and focus on ourselves. We walk a crooked trail.

The question: Actually, I have two. Who or what has claimed your focus and what does your path look like?

Chicken Scratch #2: Prevention of spiritual intimacy and true unity.

Perfection did not satisfy Lucifer. He wanted more—intimacy. One of his goals today? Block the intimate union between God and His sons and daughters. How does he accomplish this? He sends the perverse spirit to distort images of themselves and God. (For a bit of a refresher course, review the section on "Funhouse Mirrors" in Chapter Two.)

He also wants to block spiritual intimacy between believers to prevent true unity from manifesting in the earth. Why does Lucifer want to stop it? The following Scriptures reveal what happens when Christians come together in one accord:

- They rout more of the enemy. (Deut. 32:30)
- They cannot be overpowered by the enemy. (Eccl. 4:12)
- God commands His blessing. (Ps. 133)
- Jesus stands in the midst of them. (Matt. 18:20)
- They bear one another's burdens and fulfill the law of Christ. (Gal. 6:2)
- They corporately share in the grace God gives each individual. (Phil. 1:7)
- They exhort each other unto good works. (Heb. 10:24–25)
- They pray for each other and are healed. (James 5:14, 16)

I'm sure I only scratched the surface of the effects unity has on the kingdom of darkness. (No pun intended, though it certainly works.) Little wonder Lucifer strives to thwart believers from unity and intimacy. With over two hundred denominations just in America, he has kept the body of Christ separated for centuries.

The question: When will we come together, serve notice on him, and say no more?

Chicken Scratch #3: The view of men as wimps and women as amazons.

In creating man and woman, God placed within them definite male and female qualities to set them apart. Each particular sex carries these innate strengths. When the strengths become perverted, we see men turn into wimps while women turn into amazons. This is not to say men should not have a gentle and tender side to their manhood. Nor does it in any way diminish the strength and intelligence of a woman. But if men's masculinity or women's femininity become warped and distorted, they begin to move in the opposite direction. Developing a hatred of men or women, they ultimately separate themselves from the God who created them.

The question: Have you dealt with the misandry and misogyny in your own life?

Chicken Scratch #4: The three-headed serpent.

The Lord revealed that a three-headed serpent was connected to me. I did a little research and found a fascinating bit of information. One culture calls this serpent "Sirae."[61] Its purpose? To steal your years. I can certainly testify that the perverse spirit has stolen years from me. Am I the exception? No.

The question: Actually, I don't have one. I do have an exhortation from God's Word. Check out Joel chapter 2.

Chicken Scratch #5: Problems with reproductive organs.

Lucifer wants to destroy the "seed" of woman, her babies. If he can accomplish this by keeping a couple from conceiving, so much the better. Medical science has achieved major breakthroughs with regard to infertility treatments. Today, couples who lost hope hear "mama" and "daddy" from the tiny bundle in their arms.

The question: Do you know someone with fertility issues? Add this to your cache of spiritual weapons and start winning the war for them in prayer.

Chicken Scratch #6: A lot of stretching.

I know it sounds strange, but I occasionally saw it in my daughters when I prayed for them. If the perverse spirit manifested, they contorted their bodies or stretched out their limbs or both. Once free, they stopped. I suppose it makes sense in light of the fact that one of the Hebrew meanings for perverse is *to stretch*.[62] It still seems a little weird.

The question: No question from me. You might have one for the Lord.

Chicken Scratch #7: Problems with feet.

While this book has focused on the effects of the crooked serpent in our lives overall, some physical deformities may find root causes linked to a perverse spirit. (See Henry Wright's book *A More Excellent Way* for more information on spiritual causes for physical ailments.)[63] As a matter of fact, we get our term *scoliosis* from the Greek word for *crooked*, *skoleeos*.[64]

In earlier chapters, we discovered the Bible makes several references to crooked paths. Walking them can potentially lead to crooked feet. Let me share an incident with Holly when she was almost three. Concerned about the development of her feet, I asked a guest speaker at church to pray over them. The anointing suddenly hit, and she nearly danced off the floor without any effort of her own.

The next afternoon at our family prayer time, I decided to bless her feet. I put my hands on them, intending to pray. Without warning, Holly went ballistic. She cried and screamed. She tried to hit me, pinch me, and bite me. She did everything she could to get my hands off her feet. I knew immediately a demonic force was behind the attack, and I refused to let go. After warring against the perverse spirit, the frenzy stopped.

What an eye-opener! The obvious question? Why? I believe for several reasons. First, God gifted her with an incredible anointing to dance before Him. Second, He gifted her with keen prophetic wisdom. Third, He gifted her with a beautiful singing voice. That day, the perverse spirit planned to lead my three-year-old down a crooked path, perverting her divine call. What a diabolic plan! And what better way than to attack her feet. Consequently, I purposed in my heart to guard them. I blessed them many times during the next few weeks. We never had another episode.

The question: What's going on with your tippy-toes?

Chicken Scratch #8: The dream about the pit.

I wanted to skip this one, but the Lord wouldn't let me:

---- ⟳ ----

I am in a church at the end of the Sunday morning service. I watch most of the people go down to the basement. One person opens a door to a deep pit. The rest of them willingly step into this dark cavern. They close the door, and lock it from the inside. Only three escape, including an elderly couple I help rescue. Troubled and concerned for those who went into the pit, I want to help them but cannot.

The significance of the pit led me to Strong's and then to Job 33:15–28:

In a dream, in a vision of the night, when deep sleep falls upon men, while slumbering on their beds, then He opens the ears of men, and seals their instruction (vv. 15–16).

In order to turn man from his deed, and conceal pride from man, He keeps back his soul from the Pit, and his life from perishing by the sword (vv. 17–18).

Man is also chastened with pain on his bed, and with strong pain in many of his bones, so that his life abhors bread, and his soul succulent food [dainty meat]. His flesh wastes away from sight, and his bones stick out which once were not seen. Yes, his soul draws near the Pit, and his life to the executioners (vv.19–22).

If there is a message for him, a mediator, one among a thousand, to show man His uprightness, then He is gracious to him, and says, "Deliver him from going down to the Pit; I have found a ransom"; his flesh shall be young like a child's, he shall return to the days of his youth (vv. 23–25).

He shall pray to God, and He will delight in him, he shall see His face with joy, for He restores to man His righteousness. Then he looks at men and says, "I have sinned, and *perverted* what was right, and it did not profit me." He will redeem his soul from going down to the Pit, and his life shall see the light (vv. 26–28).

Although this is a long passage of Scripture, it demonstrates how the perverse spirit can lead a group of believers down a crooked path into a dark pit and what it takes to bring them out. Notice what these verses include:

Perverseness: A door opens to the perverse spirit, via pride.
Pride: Pride lifts your head up so high you can't see the pit you're walking into.
Chastening: Chastening brings correction and manifests in a variety of ways.
Pain in bones: Scripture tells us bitterness and envy cause bones to rot.
Abhor dainty meat: *Dainty* in Hebrew means *to lust*.[65]
Deliverance: God rescues.
Repentance: Godly sorrow = repentance = salvation.
(2 Corinthians 7:10–11)
Restoration: God redeems and restores.

Each point is worth pondering as we consider our own path. God's Word strongly exhorts us to judge ourselves lest we be judged (1 Peter 4:17). Now is a good time to do that.

The question: Are you on your way to the pit, in the pit, on your way out of the pit, or avoiding the pit?

This concludes the various chicken scratches I felt the Lord wanted me to share. Hopefully, you have some meat to chew on or at the very least a chicken bone; sorry, I couldn't resist. Let's turn our focus to the insightful tidbits and see what we can discover.

Insightful Tidbit #1: The chameleon.

The chameleon, a type of lizard, has the capacity to change its colors to blend into the surroundings. The perverse spirit has the capacity to look like one of its cohorts to continue its writhing, torturous path.

The question: Are you color-blind to the perverse spirit?

Insightful Tidbit #2: The underlying linchpin.

Webster's states a linchpin *holds together the elements of something complex.* Picture a stack of objects held together by a linchpin. Remove it and the objects crash to the floor. Now apply the picture to a collection of demons (pride, lying, jealousy, infirmity, or . . .) held together by their linchpin, the perverse spirit. Remove the perverse spirit, and the rest of the demons scatter.

The question: I don't have a question this time. It's more like a command: Pull that sucker out of its place and stand and see the salvation of the Lord in your life.[66]

Insightful Tidbit #3: The elusive serpent.

When I first began the warfare to enforce the defeat of the perverse spirit in my life, I couldn't seem to get a grip on him. I thought I had him under my feet, and then he popped up somewhere else in my life. For a long time, I despaired of being free. But that's not truth. Truth states I am more than a conqueror through Christ who loves me. Though I may not be where I want to be, I'm a lot farther than I used to be. The day will come when my foot crushes his neck every time, any time he tries to slither into my life.

The question: Do you have a handle on him yet? No? Don't give up. Your help is in the name of the Lord.

Insightful Tidbit #4: Food for thought.

An interesting prophecy found in Isaiah 7:14–15 tends to get overlooked when we hear messages about Jesus, especially around Christmas. Although preachers expound on verse 14, verse 15 doesn't receive much attention:

> Therefore the LORD Himself will give you a sign: Behold, the virgin shall conceive and bear a Son, and shall call His name Immanuel (v. 14).

> Curds and honey He shall eat, that He may know to refuse the evil and choose the good (v. 15).

The King James Version states verse 15 this way, "Butter and honey shall he eat, that he may know to refuse the evil, and choose the good." Seven hundred years before the birth of Jesus, Isaiah foretold what He would eat. God, the Ancient of Days, spoke *into the earth* the food the Savior of the world would eat so He could choose good over evil. Paying attention to what's on our plates is long overdue. The ramifications of this revelation have the power to change lives for eternity.

The question: What are you eating for lunch?

Insightful Tidbit #5: The Down side of life.

My friend, Heidi, has a daughter with Down syndrome. Nicole is an absolute delight. Bright, funny, and stubborn, she has an artistic element in the works. We all love her. Still, we want to see her made completely whole, without the extra chromosome 21 in her DNA. What's the connection to the perverse spirit? I didn't see one until I talked to Heidi about the manuscript. Suddenly, God dropped a revelation into my spirit, and I just about fell off my chair! Literally!

In Chapter Three, we discovered how the perverse spirit deceived Eve. She *vitiated* the Word of the Lord. Let's review the definition: *To make faulty or defective often by the addition of something that impairs.* Apply the same principle to Down syndrome. An extra chromosome 21 *vitiates* the DNA structure, impairing the baby's development, resulting in Down syndrome.

How does the perverse spirit accomplish this in the womb? We already addressed the fact that satan wants to destroy babies. If he can't kill them *in* the womb, he'll attempt to add, subtract, multiply, or divide before they *leave* the womb by causing serious birth defects. Due to extreme liberal abortion laws, the majority of babies diagnosed with Down syndrome never take their first breath.[67]

As far as the open door allowing the perverse spirit to *vitiate* the baby in the womb, two doors we previously exposed could be rejection or rebellion by the parents. On the other hand, it might be the answer Jesus gave His followers regarding the reason for the man born blind at birth. His disciples assumed either the man or the parents had sinned. The Savior held a different perspective, a heavenly insight. "Jesus answered, 'Neither this man nor his parents sinned, but that the works of God should be revealed in him'" (John 9:3).

Regardless of the reason for the open door, God wants to reveal his works in those born with Down syndrome. How do you pray in this situation? I can tell you how Heidi and I pray for Nicole. She doesn't have her complete manifestation of wholeness, yet when we pray against the perverse spirit in her body, she shows signs of improvement. Here's a sample prayer:

Lord, in Jesus' name, I take authority over the perverse spirit and bind him from operating in Nicole's life. I cover her with the blood of Jesus. The enemy has no authority over her. I command the extra chromosome 21 to drop off every DNA strand, and I declare all effects of Down syndrome null and void. As the extra chromosome 21 detaches and falls away, I speak to every part of her body to line up with the Word of God. By His stripes, she is made whole. Thank you, Father, for what you're doing in her life. What an honor to see your marvelous works manifested in Nicole. All praises to the only wise God, in Jesus' name. Amen.

The question: Does someone in your family or someone you know have Down syndrome or other birth defects? Start praying and expect to see the works of God manifest.

Insightful Tidbit #6: A bone to pick? Funny bones? Feeling it in my bones?

Remember Chicken Scratch #7? This particular tidbit follows the same path. It also carries the potential to aggravate, irritate, and possibly humiliate some individuals. A minister of the gospel actually prophesied those words over me, and though I never do it on purpose, it sometimes just happens. I simply want to give you a heads up. Check out these verses from Psalms 31 and 40:

> Have mercy on me, O LORD, for I am in trouble; my eye wastes away with grief, yes, my soul and my body! For my life is spent with grief, and my years with sighing; my strength fails because of my *iniquity*, and my bones waste away. I am a reproach among all my enemies, but especially among my neighbors, and am repulsive to my acquaintances; those who see me outside flee from me. (Ps. 31:9–11)

> My *iniquities* have overtaken me, so that I am not able to look up; they are more than the hairs of my head; therefore my heart fails me. (Ps. 40:12b)

The point? Iniquity/perverseness in a person's life can conceivably lead to detrimental effects on physical and emotional health. Those mentioned here include eyesight, strength, bones, depression, and heart trouble.

The question: Do macular degeneration, chronic fatigue syndrome, arthritis, depression or coronary heart disease find spiritual root causes hidden in iniquity and perverseness? To make sure I don't aggravate, irritate, and possibly humiliate some people, I'll leave the answer as . . .

This is the end of the insightful tidbits. I hope you found them informative and enlightening. I do feel led to give an exhortation at this point. Please, please, please don't let guilt and condemnation smother you for anything you've read thus far. Remember, the purpose of *Making Crooked Places Straight* is to expose the perverse spirit and provide training, enabling you to overcome and walk in victory. The ultimate goal? Crooked places made straight. Freedom in the Christian walk. Fulfillment in destinies. Shining like stars.

Although, you may not think yourself spiritually "savvy" or know anything about spiritual warfare, don't despair. The next chapter gives you powerful weapons to take down the enemy. Better still, the Great I AM lives on the inside of you. When you don't know how to pray, Romans 8:26 says, ". . . the Spirit Himself makes intercession for us with groanings which cannot be uttered." He picks up the slack and covers you. After all, that's what covenant partners do for each other. You never battle alone.

As we end the chapter, I'll let you judge whether this lined up with God's plan or if the chicken scratches will end up at the water cooler.

CHAPTER 6

Treading upon the Serpent

Treading on serpents? I don't think so. I don't plan on getting close to any snakes . . . Wait a minute. You're not talking about real ones; you're talking about this perverse spirit. How do you do that with this devil? I can see he's one mean, ugly sucker. And I get why you call him the granddaddy. I'll never be able to pretend he's only in the world or connected with homosexuals. Still, how do you stomp on something that big without being crushed by it?

You're right, you can't. Not on your own. But Jesus gave us His authority to do just that. Look at Luke 10:19, "Behold, I give you authority to [tread] on serpents and scorpions, and over all the *power* of the enemy, and nothing shall by any means hurt you." Did you notice what He did not say? He did not say check the size of the serpent or the scorpion before we walked all over them. He did not say His authority only worked if they were less than three feet long or two inches in diameter. He did not say to wear steel-toed reinforced boots. No. He said He gave us authority to tread on serpents and scorpions and any other kind of enemy power, regardless of the package. *Power* in this verse comes from the Greek word *dunamis* which means *supernatural, miraculous power.*[68] Jesus gave us authority to tread on that kind of power with the guarantee nothing would hurt us.

Moreover, according to Philippians 4:13, "[We] can do all things through Christ who strengthens [us]." This is a promise we do not want to forget or ignore. A quick word study will help us understand the meaning. *Strengthen*[69] has roots from the same Greek term found in Luke 10:19 for *power*. Dunamis. Supernatural, miraculous power. In essence, we can do all things through Christ, the Messiah or Anointed One, who gives us supernatural, miraculous power. In addition, we have 2 Corinthians 10:4, which states, "For the weapons of our warfare are not carnal [or of the flesh], but mighty [through] God for pulling down strongholds." According to Strong's, *mighty* is related to *dunamis.*[70] *Supernatural, miraculous power.* Without question, God wants us to understand we have His authority to walk in supernatural, miraculous power every time we deal with the enemy.

What exactly are these formidable weapons? While they don't look like the weapons our military uses to wage war, they do tear down the strongholds of the perverse spirit. Some will be familiar; others may surprise you. Before we get started, a quick reminder: *Iniquities* and *perverseness* are interchangeable. Now let's see what's in our spiritual arsenal:

Weapon #1: The blood of Jesus.

Don't ever think you can go into battle without the power of the blood of the Lamb. Cover yourself, your family, *everything* pertaining to you. Remember, the angel of death had to pass over the Israelites because of the blood of the lamb (Exodus 12:23). The same principle holds true here. The blood of Jesus, the sinless, perfect Lamb of God, is our most potent weapon against the wiles of the enemy. You do not want to forget this truth, especially when your foot comes down on the head of the serpent.

Weapon #2: The name of Jesus.

Names are exceedingly important in Scripture, and none more so than the name of Jesus. In Acts 4:8–12, Peter declared that the name of Jesus Christ of Nazareth held not just the power to heal, but also the gift of salvation. In his letter to the Philippians, Paul confirmed this great truth when he wrote that every knee will bow and every tongue will confess Jesus as Lord (2:10–11). If you tread on the perverse spirit without this revelation, you may end up like the seven sons of Sceva, running naked through the streets. Not a pretty sight. Check out Acts 19.

Weapon #3: The Word of God.

By now I sound like an annoying swarm of angry bees, but to reiterate again, words have incredible force. Whether spoken or written, the Word of God is the most powerful word in existence, both in the spiritual realm and the physical arena. According to Hebrews, God first framed the worlds by His words, and now upholds all things by the Word of His power (Hebrews 11:3; 1:3). To drive this point home, look at Hebrews 4:12, "For the word of God is living and powerful, and sharper than any two-edged sword, piercing even to the division of soul and spirit, and of joints and marrow, and is a discerner of the thoughts and intents of the heart."

A passage in Psalms leaves no room to debate the massive power at work through God's word:

> . . . because of their transgression, and because of their *iniquities*, [they] were afflicted. Their soul[s] abhorred all manner of food, and they drew near to the gates of death. Then they cried out to the LORD in their trouble, and He saved them out of their distresses. He sent His word and healed them, and delivered them from their destructions. (Ps. 107:17–20)

I think the psalmist had a brilliant idea when he hid God's Word in his heart (Psalm 119:11). Talk about a secret weapon! One word can lead to a complete rout of the enemy in our lives. If you haven't started to hide Scripture in your heart, I'd do double time on this one. Treading on the enemy with a Bible verse turns into a cakewalk because it only takes one word from heaven's throne. Just one word.

Weapon #4: The laughter of God.

Laughter and joy. Do you realize the Scriptures refer to a form of them nearly eight hundred times? (No, I did not count each one; thank God for Bible computer programs.) The Lord inspired the writers of the Old and New Testaments to include admonitions, instructions, and sometimes out and out commands, to walk in joy, rejoice, be glad, laugh, be happy, and delight ourselves in Him. Yet, today many ignore, disregard, or blame the devil when it happens in our Christian meetings. At the very least, we need to know what tickles God's funny bone. Psalm 2:4 gives us the answer, "He who sits in the heavens shall laugh; the LORD shall hold [his enemies] in derision."

If God Almighty laughs at His enemies, wouldn't it be appropriate for His sons and daughters to do likewise? Unfortunately, the joy of the Lord and laughter in the church receive severe criticism, even resulting in splits. Open door #4, anyone?

In spite of various ploys of the adversary to keep it out of our gatherings, laughter releases a powerful blast against the perverse spirit. Why don't you let some giggles, chuckles, or belly laughs spill out as your feet come down on the neck of the enemy? Meanwhile, God won't be sitting still. He can straighten a lot of crooked places when His joy overflows.

Weapon #5: The wisdom of God.

Numerous passages warn against the perverse spirit. Proverbs 2:10–15 specifically relates the importance of wisdom in delivering us from the wiles of this crooked serpent:

> When wisdom enters your heart, and knowledge is pleasant to your soul, discretion will preserve you; understanding will keep you,
> to deliver you from the way of evil, from the man who speaks *perverse* things,
> from those who leave the paths of uprightness to walk in the ways of darkness;
> who rejoice in doing evil, and delight in the *perversity* of the wicked;
> whose ways are *crooked*, and who are devious in their paths . . .

If you haven't prayed for the wisdom of God, I wouldn't let any more grass grow under your feet. You might find a perverse spirit slithering between your toes.

Weapon #6: The peace of God.

Surprisingly, the *shalom* peace of God turns out to be a powerful weapon. In Chapter Two, we discovered *shalom* in Hebrew means *to be completed; nothing missing, nothing broken, everything made whole.*[71] Not only does this weapon mend breaches resulting from perverse words, it destroys the enemy, "And the God of peace will crush Satan under your feet shortly . . ." (Romans 16:20). Our armor includes feet shod with peace (Ephesians 6:15). If you know anything about Roman warriors, their boots weren't made just for walking. Yours shouldn't be either.

Weapon #7: The truth of God.

In earlier chapters, we discovered God's truth to be a formidable weapon. In the Gospel of John, Jesus said to those who believed Him, "And you shall know the truth, and the truth shall make you free" (John 8:32). Truth, in and of itself, cannot set someone free. Truth, known and experienced beyond accepted facts, brings freedom to those in bondage. Interestingly, Pilate asked Jesus the question, "What is truth?" He would have been better served had he asked Him this question, "Who is truth?" Why? Because a few hours earlier, Jesus gave His disciples the precise definition of truth, one still causing an uproar in the world today:

> I am the way, the truth, and the life. No one comes to the Father except through Me. . . . And I will pray the Father, and He will give you another Helper, that He may abide with you forever—the Spirit of truth . . . (John 14:6, 16–17a)

David sought truth when he cried out to God after his own *iniquity* (*perverseness*) was uncovered, "Behold, You desire truth in the inward parts, and in the hidden part You will make me to know wisdom" (Ps. 51:6). God desires truth in our inner man to replace areas made crooked by our iniquities. Only His truth, and His alone, can make them straight. Keep this weapon handy while treading upon the crooked serpent.

Weapon #8: The righteousness of God.

This unexpected weapon holds amazing properties:

> . . . But righteousness delivers from death. (Prov. 10:2)

> . . . Revive me in Your righteousness. (Ps. 119:40)

Delivered from death and revived in His righteousness. And for the record, *revive* doesn't only mean to become alert. Other definitions include *to nourish, preserve, recover, repair, be whole.*[72] Don't treat this weapon like a squirt gun! When you fully understand your righteousness in Christ Jesus, it transforms into a water cannon, keeping the enemy under your feet. The only place he's supposed to be!

Weapon #9: The mercy of God.

According to Scripture, His mercy includes multiple strategies:

> Who is a God like You, pardoning *iniquity* and passing over the transgression of the remnant of His heritage? He does not retain His anger forever, because He delights in mercy. He will again have compassion on us, and will subdue our *iniquities.* (Micah 7:18–19)

> In mercy and truth atonement is provided for *iniquity.* (Prov. 16:6)

> If I say, "My foot slips," Your mercy, O LORD, will hold me up. (Ps. 94:18)
> (Remember the section on backsliding?)

But He, being full of compassion, forgave their *iniquity*, and did not destroy them. Yes, many a time He turned His anger away, and did not stir up all His wrath; for He remembered that they were but flesh, a breath that passes away and does not come again. (Ps. 78:38–39)

Oh, do not remember former *iniquities* against us! Let Your tender mercies come speedily to meet us, for we have been brought very low. (Ps. 79:8)

O Israel, hope in the LORD; for with the LORD there is mercy, and with Him is abundant redemption. And He shall redeem Israel from all his *iniquities*. (Ps. 130:7–8)

This incredible weapon carries firepower beyond our imagination!

A look at Strong's provides added depth to this warhead. *Mercy* is the Hebrew covenant word *kheh-sed*.[73] *Agape,* the Greek counterpart, translates to our English equivalent for *love*.[74] Due to the vastness of what *mercy* carries in the spirit, I cannot do justice in this book describing what God did for us through His *kheh-sed/agape love*. (For those who want to pursue it, I highly recommend Kenneth Copeland's teaching on the Blood Covenant, an excellent resource!)[75] I will tell you this: When we go to war against the perverse spirit, God doesn't play patty-cake with His *kheh-sed/agape love*, trying to make us feel better. He uses it to subdue our iniquities (Micah 7:19b). The Hebrew word for *subdue* means *to tread down and to conquer*.[76] Romans 8:37 states that we are more than conquerors through Christ who *kheh-sed/agape loves* us. According to 1 Corinthians 13:8, this weapon never, never, never fails. If that isn't enough, His *kheh-sed/agape love*, along with truth, provides atonement for iniquity (Proverbs 16:6). A weapon of this caliber is an absolute necessity. Any time, every time, all the time we walk on enemy turf.

Weapon #10: The fear of God.

Oh, what delight, what rest, what victory we find in the fear of the Lord! Malachi 4 declares not only are we healed, but we will walk upon those who do wickedly and work iniquity:

> "For behold, the day is coming, burning like
> an oven,
> and all the proud, yes, all who do *wickedly*
> will be stubble.
> And the day which is coming shall burn them
> up,"
> says the LORD of hosts,
> "that will leave them neither root nor branch.
> But to you
> who *fear My name* . . . You shall trample
> [tread down] the *wicked*,
> for they shall be ashes under the soles of
> your feet . . ."
> (Mal 4:1, 2a, 3a. Note that wicked and iniquity
> are related in Strong's.)[77]

Lest we forget, the wicked are not flesh and blood. They are not spouses, relatives, coworkers, employers, neighbors, or other members of the human race. In his letter to the Ephesians, Paul wrote, "For we do not wrestle against flesh and blood, but against principalities, against powers, against the rulers of the darkness of this age, against spiritual hosts of wickedness in the heavenly places" (Ephesians 6:12). But ashes under our feet? I can't think of a better place for a wicked, perverse spirit to be. How about you?

Weapon #11: The grace of God.

Although we saw the importance of God's grace in Chapter One, it bears another look. To refresh your memory, God's grace brings down mountains (Zechariah 4:7), raises a barrier to ward off the enemy (2 Corinthians 12:9), and rescues us from a life without God (Ephesians 2:8). No one can survive an onslaught of the perverse spirit without the grace of God. Don't even try.

Weapon #12: The armor of God.

Ephesians 6 describes the various pieces of God's armor:

- Belt of truth
- Breastplate of righteousness
- Preparation of peace for our feet
- Helmet of salvation
- Shield of faith
- Sword of the Spirit

With the glory of God as our rear guard (Isaiah 52:12), and His angels keeping charge over us (Psalm 91:11–12), our covering is complete. The armor of God. Don't leave home without it. Don't go into battle without it. The damage incurred won't be worth it. Cover up and start trampling!

Weapon #13: The spirit of adoption and sonship.

Relatively unknown, the revelation of this weapon can bring utmost freedom. Paul referred to it twice:

> For as many as are led by the Spirit of God, these are sons of God. For you did not receive the spirit of bondage again to fear, but you received *the Spirit of adoption* by whom we cry out, "Abba, Father." The Spirit Himself bears witness with our spirit that we are children of God, and if children, then heirs—heirs of God and joint heirs with Christ . . . (Rom. 8:14–17a)

> And because you are sons, God has sent forth the *Spirit of His Son (sonship)* into your hearts, crying out, "Abba, Father!" Therefore you are no longer a slave but a son, and if a son, then an heir of God through Christ. (Gal. 4:6–7)

No longer slaves, but sons of the Most High God! When we grasp the truth that we have a Father who loves us and wants us, we experience indescribable joy! Our Father calls us by our names (Isaiah 43:1), engraves our images into the palms of His hands (Isaiah 49:16), and proclaims us as the apple of His eye (Psalm 17:8). Not one crooked path can be found, not one crooked path can remain. Our Abba Daddy leads the way, and His path is never crooked. Never.

Weapon #14: The offense not taken.

Simple, but mighty, and possibly an odd duck in our list of weapons. *Offense* comes from the Greek word, *skandalon*, which originates from a simple method of snaring animals.[78] Over time, the word came to mean an offense. Comparing the natural to the spiritual, we see a clear picture of how the enemy uses offenses to trip people up and cause them to stumble again and again. Caught in a trap, we find ourselves in a backslidden state on a very crooked path. The Highway of Holiness appears only as a speck on the distant horizon (Isaiah 35).

Our weapon? Choose not to take an offense. You may think a little offense is not a big deal. Jesus thought differently:

> But [Jesus] turned and said to Peter, "Get behind Me, Satan! You are an offense to Me, for you are not mindful of the things of God, but the things of men." (Matt. 16:23)

> Woe to the world because of offenses! For offenses must come, but woe to that man by whom the offense comes! (Matt. 18:7)

Adamant His disciples not be offended, He continued His warning in the next verse. He told His disciples to cut off a body part if it caused them to sin. Highly drastic measures! Matthew's version makes no mistake in the context. Offenses. Why so harsh? Unforgiveness and bitterness lead to a crooked path. Paul prayed for the saints in Philippi to be *sincere and without offense*

(Philippians 1:10). I urge you to make it your prayer too. This not-so-little weapon is probably a size eighteen!

Weapon #15: The deliverance of God.

No one wants to think about the need for deliverance from a perverse spirit. Honestly, no one wants to think about deliverance at all. Yet, Jesus used this weapon multiple times during His ministry with outstanding results:

- Daughter of the Syro-Phoenician woman delivered. (Mark 7:25–30)
- Demons cast out throughout Galilee. (Mark 1:39)
- Demons cast out with a word. (Matt. 8:16)
- Epileptic son delivered. (Mark 9:14–27)
- Mute boy speaks. (Matt. 9:32–33)
- The demoniac delivered. (Mark 5:1–15)

The perverse spirit counts on you to shy away from using this firearm. Don't give him the satisfaction. Let him experience the terror of the Lion of Judah roaring from your spirit and send him to the footstool of Jesus. You'll experience a new level of freedom you never thought possible.

Weapon #16: The work of the cross.

Much has been said and much has been written about the cross. Rather than a lengthy discourse about Jesus' accomplishments on the cross, I'm going to zero in on a few verses found in Isaiah 53.

Verse 5 says, "But He was wounded for our transgressions, He was bruised for our iniquities . . ." The transgressions mentioned in the first portion of this verse aren't little white lies we say to cover up our true feelings. These translate from the Hebrew as *rebellion on a governmental level, a moral level, and a spiritual level.*[79] According to Isaiah's prophecy, Jesus was pierced due to our rebellion against God's government in our lives, against the moral compass of God's law in our lives, and against God's spiritual covering over our lives.

How do you tread on the perverse spirit in light of this revelation? Obedience. Every time you obey, you stomp all over the ugly sucker. Every time you walk in rebellion in any of those three arenas, you follow a crooked path. I don't know about you, but I'm going to choose obedience and make sure the perverse spirit knows what kind of boots I wear.

As for the second part of the verse, look closer at those bruises. They resulted from internal bleeding caused by outward physical blows. Jesus suffered tremendous hits to His body. While blood poured out from the lashes and the spikes, massive bleeding gushed through His internal organs. What exactly did those bruises accomplish? In essence, they allowed our iniquities, the crooked places in our lives, to be made straight.

Verse 6 clearly states what the Lord required of Jesus on the cross, "All we like sheep have gone astray; we have turned, every one, to his own way; and the LORD has laid on [Jesus] the *iniquity* of us all." Not only was He bruised for our iniquities, but God put the entire burden of the iniquity of every single person on Jesus while He hung on the cross.

Still not satisfied, Isaiah continues in verses 11–12, looking ahead at the finished work of the cross:

He shall see the labor of His soul, and be satisfied. By His knowledge My righteous Servant shall justify many, for He shall bear their iniquities (v. 11).

Therefore I will divide Him a portion with the great, and He shall divide the spoil with the strong, because He poured out His soul unto death, and He was numbered with the transgressors, and He bore the sin of many, and made intercession for the transgressors (v. 12).

As I write, the magnificent love of our Savior overwhelms me. How can we not give Him our all? Everything we are, everything we have, everything we hope to be is all because of Jesus! As we dance in adoration at the foot of the cross, let our feet enforce the defeat the Savior of mankind won for us as He cried out, "It is finished!"

Weapon #17: The power of forgiveness.

While rebellion and rejection open the door to the perverse spirit, unforgiveness gives him the title deed to set up residence. He actually relishes the thought of decorating the walls of our temples with framed quotes from wounded pasts. And make no mistake, he thoroughly enjoys replaying the memories of arguments, betrayals, and pain we experienced on the screen of our imagination. Day after day he warps the images we see of ourselves, others, and God.

Obviously, our weapon to destroy his squatting rights is forgiveness. Yet, millions of people stare at the decorated walls and watch re-runs of the past, preferring bondage over liberty. The problem? We don't want to forgive. We'll hold onto grudges instead of walking in freedom. I'm reminded of an incident that happened years ago.

One summer, I needed the alternator in my car replaced. I managed to scrounge up the funds for the part, but had no extra money for the labor. A fellow brother in Christ offered to fix it, but he wanted payment. I explained my financial dilemma and asked him if twenty-five dollars would be enough. He responded, "It'll do."

Two weeks later he called me. "I'd like to come by and get another twenty-five dollars for the work I did on your car."

"Oh," I said. "OK. I won't have the money until the end of the week."

"I'll stop by on Friday."

We ended the call, and rage spilled out. I could not believe he demanded more cash when he knew my circumstances. Daily the conversation replayed in my mind. When he showed up on the appointed day, I handed over money I actually needed for groceries. He couldn't look at me, which was a good thing, since my blazing eyes would have roasted him on a barbecue skewer. Throughout the rest of the summer, I couldn't let go of my anger. Every day I thought of a new way to punish him.

In the middle of September, a local ministry hosted a guest speaker for special meetings. At the end of one session, I saw a vision unfold:

I'm carrying a pure white bag the size of a small Volkswagen on my back. Because of its weight, I'm completely bent over. I glance up to see Jesus about ten feet away.

"Penelope, I want you to forgive him."

I know exactly which person He's referring to. "No."

"You need to forgive him."

"I don't want to."

"You can't carry this burden anymore. It's too heavy."

"I don't care. I'm not going to forgive him."

"Why not?"

"Because I know you. You're going to do absolutely nothing about this. You'll let him off scot-free. I'm a single mom, and he knows I don't have extra money. Even after I gave him the first twenty-five dollars, the slimebucket called me up and demanded more. He deserves everything he gets!"

"Penelope, give Me that burden."

"I said no!"

By now, Jesus appears slightly annoyed with me, but I don't care about that either. This bag is too important. I have spent hours buffing and polishing it to make sure it stays clean without any spots or wrinkles. My burden is righteous, and I'm not about to let it go. For the next several minutes, we argue back and forth, our tempers starting to flare. We finally reach the point of yelling.

"Look! I want to bless you, and I can't as long as you won't give it to Me! Let Me have it."

"Fine!" The words spit out of my mouth like a machine gun. "You want it, you can have it!" In spite of its size, I manage to throw the bag so hard that it knocks Jesus to the ground. We stare at each other with stunned looks. Then we start to laugh.

Although the anger and unforgiveness vanished, the joy remained. I forgave my brother in Christ, and Jesus thoroughly blessed me in the meetings. Had

I held onto my self-righteous grudge, I would have missed all God wanted to do for me, through me, and in me. The perverse spirit would have robbed me, but not as a victim, instead as a willing accomplice.

If unforgiveness has found a place in your heart, don't wait one second more. Forgive! Yes, they were wrong. Yes, they destroyed your finances. Yes, they left permanent scars on your body. Yes, they violated your trust. Yes, Yes, and Yes. But without forgiveness, the quotes on the walls of your temple will continue to mock you and the memories will haunt you. Take it to the cross and let forgiveness cleanse your spirit, soul, and body. In the meantime, the perverse spirit will end up behind permanent lock and key—exactly where he needs to be.

Weapon #18: The divine exchange of crowns.

Crowns. People die for them. People kill for them. Wars are fought over them. Nations rise and fall because of them. Yet, the most important crown in the history of humanity sat, not on a conquering king, but on a condemned man. No ordinary man stood before Pilate. The Savior of the world held the world in his hands that long ago Passover morning. When Roman soldiers jammed the crown of thorns onto the head of Jesus, they had no idea of the ramifications set to spiral down through the ages.

As the twisted thorns penetrated his scalp—and the key here is *twisted*—a divine exchange occurred. The Son wore the thorny crown; the Father gave us the mind of Christ. Jesus willingly exchanged His pure, righteous thoughts for our twisted, perverted ones.

What an astounding revelation! No more anguish in our minds. No more haunting images from the past. No more warped thinking. The battle in the mind is over! Crowned with remarkable fire power, the mind of Christ directs our thoughts, leads our steps, and motivates our actions.

If you struggle with tormenting thoughts, pick up this weapon and fire it dead on at the perverse spirit. Remind him of the cross. Remind him of the divine exchange of crowns. Remind him that you have the mind of Christ. Daily see yourself with the crown of God's lovingkindness and tender mercies resting upon your head (Psalm 103:4). His supernatural power vanquishes the enemy because of the crown you wear. We are truly more than conquerors through Christ who loves us. The book of Revelation declares us to be His kings and priests (1:6). With His crown on your head, step into your authority and walk all over the slippery snake.

Weapon #19: The perfect walk.

The world leads us to believe the perfect walk happens when someone walks on the red carpet. Definitely a far cry from what Scripture states. Psalm 101 refers to a perfect walk:

I will behave wisely in a perfect way. Oh when will You come to me? I will walk within my house with a perfect heart (v. 2).

I will set nothing wicked before my eyes . . . (v. 3a).

A *perverse* heart [spirit] shall depart from me; I will not know wickedness (v. 4).

We all know "walking the walk" is easier said than done. This one is no exception. According to the psalmist, we have to:

- Behave wisely and do it perfectly
- Walk in our house with a perfect heart
- Purposely not look at anything wicked

A rather impossible predicament, don't you think? Furthermore, since we believers tend to attempt this in our own strength or do it our own way, the question isn't "if" we'll fail, but "when" we'll fail. Why? In spite of Frank Sinatra's famous rendition, doing things your own way is the epitome of rebellion, a wide open door for a perverse spirit to run amok in a person's life.

Yet, how do we walk perfectly in our own homes? Let me share a personal story. Many years ago, I received some deliverance. In order to walk it out, God required perfection from me. I knew He didn't actually expect perfection because, well, because. Keenly aware of how incapable I was of fulfilling His requirement, I couldn't wrap my brain around this directive from the Lord.

As I drove home, pondering my dilemma, God suddenly dropped the revelation into my spirit. My perfection came not from my own flawed attempts to be perfect, but from my life hidden in Christ, the perfect, sinless Lamb (Colossians 3:3). As long as I lived my life in Him, I could walk in my house with a perfect heart in a perfect way all day, every day. My only requirement? *Set nothing wicked before my eyes.* Incredible relief of not having to be perfect anymore as well as tremendous gratitude for a way of escape from the bondage of perfection poured over me in the car that day. Hidden in Christ *is* the perfect walk because He is Perfection. It's exactly how we tread on the perverse spirit. Walking in Christ. All-encompassing perfection. It just doesn't get any more perfect.

Weapon #20: The power of prayer.

Prayer. The Bible records hundreds of instances of people praying. Kings, priests, prophets, warriors, prostitutes, shepherds, farmers, mothers, and widows—all lifted their voices to the throne of Jehovah God.

These examples and more demonstrate the power of prayer. James wrote, "The effective, fervent prayer of a righteous man *avails* much" (5:16b). The word *avails* means *to exercise force.*[80] I think it's past time that we realize our prayers are weapons of mass destruction and exercise divine force. Turn your sights on the perverse spirit and stop him dead in his tracks.

Weapon #21: The scepter of righteousness in the land.

Land. Everyone wants a little piece to stake their claim and call their own. Why? I believe it's part of our spiritual DNA. Genesis, the book of beginnings, gives us clarity:

- Gen 1:1–10: God created land on Day 3, only after He created light and the heavens.
- Gen 1:26, 2:7: God created Adam, His image and likeness on earth, from the land.

- Gen 2:8: God planted a garden and gave Adam charge over it.
- Gen 3:17–19: God cursed the land because of Adam's sin.
- Gen 8:21: God vowed to not curse the land after the flood, in spite of the wickedness of man's imagination.
- Gen 15:18: God cut a covenant with Abraham and gave him a covenant promise concerning the land he would inherit.

Clearly, land holds great value in God's eyes. When Israel committed abominations in the sight of the Lord, such as child sacrifice and temple prostitution to pagan deities, the people went into bondage and lost their land. So with that in mind, Psalm 125 gives us another weapon:

> For the scepter of wickedness shall not rest on the land allotted to the righteous, lest the righteous reach out their hands to *iniquity*. Do good, O Lord, to those who are good, and to those who are upright in their hearts. As for such as turn aside to their *crooked* ways, the Lord shall lead them away with the workers of *iniquity* . . . (vv. 3–5a).

According to verse 3, a scepter of wickedness over the land tempts God's righteous seed to take hold of *iniquity* and *perverseness*. You won't have to wait for the door to open; you'll be holding hands with the perverse spirit wherever you walk. Eventually, a throne of *iniquity* gains ascendancy (Psalm 94:20). To prevent that from happening, a scepter of righteousness must rest over the land allotted to us.

How do we effectively wield this scepter? First and foremost, know your authority as a believer. Second, find as much information as you can about the history of the land allotted to you. Third, seek the Lord in prayer and/or fasting for the specific tactic He wants you to employ. A number of strategies for praying over the land have emerged in the last few years, including the following:

- Carrying out a Jericho march on the land. (Joshua 6)
- Interceding over the land. This includes, but is not limited to, weeping and travailing, the roarings of the Lord (the Lion of the Tribe of Judah),

making decrees and declarations, and performing various prophetic acts, all under the unction of Holy Spirit. (Romans 8:21–22)

- Praying and interceding for government leaders in authority over the land. (1 Timothy 2:1–2)
- Prophesying over the land. (Jeremiah 22:29)
- Redeeming the land. This particular strategy can involve communion as well as anointing with oil. (Leviticus 25:23–34)
- Repentance for wickedness committed on the land. This includes idolatry, shedding innocent blood, immorality, and breaking covenants. (2 Chronicles 7:14)
- Sanctifying the land. (Leviticus 27:17–25)
- Staking the land. (Isaiah 33:20)

Once you have the plan, don't wait any longer. Start treading on the serpent. The land has been waiting for you.

Weapon #22: The praise and worship of God.

Definitely a surprise here, praise and worship performs double duty—glorifies the Great I AM and binds the enemy. Psalm 149 shows just how powerful this weapon is:

Let the saints be joyful in glory;
Let them sing aloud on their beds.
Let the high praises of God be in their mouth,
And a two-edged sword in their hand,
To execute vengeance on the nations,
And punishments on the peoples;
To bind their kings with chains,
And their nobles with fetters of iron;
To execute on them the written judgment—
This honor have all His saints.
Praise the LORD! (vv. 5–9)

Every person washed in the blood of Jesus gets to execute judgment on the perverse spirit with their praise and worship. As a result, the enemy's effectiveness is no better than a rabbit stuck to a tar baby. Don't wait until you're in church. Open your heart, open your mouth and lift up your voice to the King of kings. Then watch the high praises bind the crooked serpent and render him completely useless.

Weapon #23: The power of unity.

Unity among people is a force even God had to reckon with regarding the tower of Babel, ". . . now nothing that they propose to do will be withheld from them" (Genesis 11:6b). One of the chicken scratches in Chapter Five went into detail about the power of unity, so I won't belabor the point. However, as a reminder of just how much clout we carry together, consider the following:

- Walls fall down. (Josh. 6:20)
- Buildings shake. (Acts 4:31)
- Prison doors open. (Acts 12)

This weapon is no toy gun. Take the fire power of unity and blast the slithering serpent into oblivion.

Weapon #24: The anointing of God.

Who doesn't desire to walk in, stand in, prophesy in, preach in, and worship in the anointing of God? While we bask in waves of glory, we don't realize what a powerful weapon we have available to us. According to Isaiah 10:27, the anointing removes the burden and destroys the yoke. Yet, this experience doesn't come at our whim, and we can at times take it for granted. Only by spending time seeking God's face, worshiping Him in abandonment, and sitting at His feet in adoration do we receive the fullness of His anointing.

When those moments manifest, the perverse spirit has no more power than a BB rolling around in an empty cereal box. If you haven't spent the time cultivating this intimate relationship, start now—right now. As His anointing flows over you like a cool refreshing waterfall, the burden of this slippery serpent will be destroyed, the yoke around your neck will be obliterated, and you will never be the same.

Weapon #25: The confession and repentance of a believer.

Admit guilt. Think differently. What a novel thought for some Christian circles! Taking responsibility for sin, confessing it as sin, and changing the way you think so you won't sin. Wow! According to Scripture, if God's people willingly confess their *iniquities* (*perverse* actions and thoughts) and change the way they think, then God will not only forgive them, but heal them as well. A number of verses are very specific:

> But if they confess their *iniquity* and the *iniquity* of their fathers, with their unfaithfulness . . . and that they also have walked contrary to Me . . . if their uncircumcised hearts are humbled, and they accept their guilt—then I will remember My covenant with Jacob, and My covenant with Isaac and My covenant with Abraham I will remember . . . (Lev. 26:40, 41b–42a)

> I acknowledged my sin to You, and my *iniquity* I have not hidden. I said, "I will confess my transgressions to the LORD," and You forgave the *iniquity* of my sin. For this cause everyone who is godly shall pray to You in a time when You may be found . . . (Ps. 32:5–6a)

> For I will declare my *iniquity*; I will be in anguish over my sin. But my enemies are vigorous and they are strong . . . Do not forsake me, O LORD; O my God, be not far from me! Make haste to help me, O LORD, my salvation. (Ps. 38:18–19a, 21–22)

> Have mercy upon me, O God, according to Your lovingkindness; according to the multitude of Your tender mercies, blot out my transgressions. Wash me thoroughly from my *iniquity*, and cleanse me from my sin. For I acknowledge my transgressions, and my sin

is always before me . . . Restore to me the joy of Your salvation, and uphold me by Your generous Spirit. Then I will teach transgressors Your ways, and sinners shall be converted to You. (Ps. 51:1–3, 12–13)

Therefore, O king [Nebuchadnezzar], let my advice be acceptable to you; break off your sins by being righteous, and your *iniquities* by showing mercy to the poor. (Dan. 4:27a)
(Note: We know the king refused Daniel's advice and, a year later, was driven from men and ate grass like an ox. When he confessed and repented, God restored him to his right mind and to his kingdom.)

Nevertheless the solid foundation of God stands, having this seal: "The Lord knows those who are His," and "Let everyone who names the name of Christ depart from *iniquity*."(2 Tim. 2:19)

Confession and repentance. A simple weapon of tremendous magnitude! Confess the sin, change the way you think, and walk all over the perverse spirit. God is more than willing. But for this weapon to be effective, He's waiting on you. What are you waiting for?

Weapon #26: Just because.

How many times have you heard someone say, "Just because," in response to a question? No reason. No explanation. Just because. Our last weapon is just that—Just because. Reading through various Scriptures, the number of passages where God heals and forgives our *iniquities* and *perverseness* "just because" surprised me. The following verses need to be in our arsenal:

Blessed is he whose transgression is forgiven, whose sin is covered. Blessed is the man to whom the LORD does not impute *iniquity*. (Ps. 32:1–2)
(Paul quotes this passage in Romans 4:7.)

You have forgiven the *iniquity* of Your people; You have covered all their sin. Selah (Ps. 85:2)

Bless the LORD, O my soul; and all that is within me, bless His holy name! . . . Who forgives all your *iniquities*, who heals all your diseases . . . He has not dealt with us according to our sins, nor punished us according to our *iniquities*. (Ps. 103:1, 3, 10)

Direct my steps by Your word, and let no *iniquity* have dominion over me. (Ps. 119:133)

And the inhabitant [of the land] will not say, "I am sick"; the people who dwell in it will be forgiven their *iniquity*. (Isa. 33:24)

Speak comfort to Jerusalem, and cry out to her, that her warfare is ended, that her *iniquity* is pardoned; for she has received from the LORD's hand double for all her sins. (Isa. 40:2)

For I will forgive their *iniquity*, and their sin I will remember no more. (Jer. 31:34b)
(Quoted as a fulfillment of prophecy in Hebrews 8:12 and 10:17.)

I will cleanse them from all their *iniquity* by which they have sinned against Me, and I will pardon all their *iniquities* by which they have sinned and by which they have transgressed against Me. (Jer. 33:8)

Thus says the LORD God: "On the day that I cleanse you from all your *iniquities*, I will also enable you to dwell in the cities, and the ruins shall be rebuilt. (Ezek. 36:33)

I will heal their *backsliding*, I will love them freely, for My anger has turned away from [them]. (Hosea 14:4)

The law of truth was in his mouth, and injustice was not found on his lips. He walked with Me in peace and equity, and turned many away from *iniquity*. (Mal. 2:6)
(Peter quotes this verse as a fulfilled prophecy of Jesus in Acts 3:26.)

Looking for . . . Jesus Christ, who gave Himself for us, that He might redeem us from all [*iniquity*] and purify for Himself His own special people, zealous for good works. (Titus 2:13–14)

Just because. Some weapon, don't you think? When you're losing your grip and bone-weary from the battle, remember these two words: Just because. Just because God is who He is, you have the power to tread upon the serpent. Let out a shout while you're trampling and keep that sucker under your feet. If he has the gall to ask why, you tell him, "Just because."

With more than twenty weapons in our arsenal, you might wonder which one to use. If you're in a major attack right now, you will be tempted to throw all of them at the perverse spirit. I suggest you pray, seek the Lord, fast if you feel led, and get the mind of Christ. He knows exactly which one will get the slithering serpent under your feet. Don't forget, no matter which one He tells you to use, we have His promise in Isaiah 54:17, "'No weapon formed against you shall prosper, and every tongue which rises against you in judgment you shall condemn. This is the heritage of the servants of the LORD, and their righteousness is from Me,' says the LORD." A Yes and Amen promise He won't ignore, brush aside, or forget. Count on it!

To bring this chapter to a close, yes, the perverse spirit is the granddaddy of them all, and he is one mean, ugly sucker. I firmly believe he is a key principality loosed upon the earth today. The Lord desires to draw His bride, the church, into deeper intimacy with Him. The devil's counterfeit leads believers away from God to twisted, ungodly relationships with other people.

Moreover, I believe the perverse spirit will be instrumental in the coming apostasy. In Matthew, Jesus described the signs of the end times, "And because *iniquity* shall abound, the love of many will wax cold" (24:12 KJV).

Newer translations use *lawlessness* instead of *iniquity* (AMP, CSB, ESV, HCSB, among others). Lawlessness. People having no laws or making laws unto themselves. Remember, the book of Judges? The Israelites repeatedly did right according to their own eyes, and consequently, turned their backs on God. Several hundred years later, Isaiah prophesied severe judgment to all who call evil good and good evil:

> Woe to those who call evil good, and good evil . . . Therefore, as the fire devours the stubble, and the flame consumes the chaff, so their root will be as rottenness and their blossom will ascend like dust; because they have rejected the law of the LORD of hosts, and despised the word of the Holy One of Israel. (Isa. 5:20, 24)

God inspired Paul to write about these last days in his letters to Timothy:

> Now the Spirit expressly says that in latter times some will depart from the faith, giving heed to deceiving spirits and doctrines of demons, speaking lies in hypocrisy, having their own conscience seared with a hot iron . . . (1 Tim. 4:1–2)

> But know this, that in the last days perilous times will come: For men will be lovers of themselves, lovers of money, boasters, proud, blasphemers, disobedient to parents, unthankful, unholy, unloving, unforgiving, slanderers, without self-control, brutal, despisers of good, traitors, headstrong, haughty, lovers of pleasure rather than lovers of God . . . (2 Tim. 3:1–4)

The first chapter in his epistle to the Romans echoed similar thoughts regarding those who deliberately chose perverted, twisted thinking over truth and righteousness. And now a few millennia down the road, we see this perfectly mirrored today. Like it or not, this is our world, a *crooked* and *perverse* generation. We rub elbows every day with men and women who fit

Paul's description. In 1 Peter 2:18, the apostle tells us to submit to *froward* masters. How, then, do we live?

The church in Philippi provides a good example. A relatively small group of believers, they lived under Roman rule. Surrounded by pagan deities, they had received the good news of the gospel with joy. They remained faithful to Paul, at times his only supporters. Consequently, the apostle felt a strong bond with this church. He wrote to them with great affection, full of joy. At one point during his exhortation, he told his beloved brethren how to conduct themselves in the midst of a *crooked* and *perverse* generation. Advice we can take to heart and apply to our own lives. Spend time meditating on the verses from Philippians 2:

Therefore, my beloved, as you have always obeyed, not as in my presence only, but now much more in my absence, work out your own salvation with fear and trembling (v. 12);

For it is God who works in you both to will and to do for His good pleasure (v. 13).

Do all things without complaining and disputing (v. 14),

That you may become blameless and harmless, children of God without fault in the midst of a *crooked* and *perverse* generation, among whom you shine as lights [stars] in the world, holding fast the word of life . . . (vv. 15–16a).

Words to live by then; words to live by today.

Now back to your original question: *How do you stomp on something that big without being crushed by it?* I'm reminded of a song I learned years ago:

Sweet Victory[81]
You shall tread on the head of the serpent and the snake.
You shall tread on the scorpion, and he shall quake!

You'll rise up in power with no defeat,
and your victory will be sweet, sweet!

You shall cast out devils and you'll heal the sick!
You'll speak with new tongues, be sharp and be quick!
You'll rise up in power with no defeat,
and your victory will be sweet, sweet!

You shall be the head and not the tail.
There's just no way that you can fail!
With the greater One there's no defeat,
and victory will be sweet, sweet!

The answer? Simple. Tread on him and enjoy your sweet victory!

CHAPTER 7

The Last Word . . . Maybe

Wow! You mean there's still more? You've given me so much to think about already! Not that I'm ungrateful. Here I am, involved in my church, doing all this good work, and still my life has been as crooked as a rattler in a cactus patch. But if you have one last word, I have ears to hear.

Then, I hope you hear the echoes of a phrase I repeated again and again—plans and purposes. God determines a divine destiny for each one of us, "'For I know the thoughts that I think toward you,' says the LORD, 'thoughts of peace and not of evil, to give you a future and a hope'" (Jeremiah 29:11). He designs them specifically for each unique soul to fulfill. Still, we all have choices, the benefits of a free will.

Throughout this book, we discovered numerous characteristics of the perverse spirit. We looked at open doors allowing him access. We prayed many prayers of forgiveness and repentance. We discovered an arsenal of weapons to help us secure the victory Jesus obtained for us on the cross. Now, with great joy, we see ourselves moving toward fulfilling our purposes. Yet, countless believers fall short of their God-ordained callings. How does a destiny get skewed? Obviously, major attacks of rejection or deep-seated rebellion take people on crooked paths of ungodly proportions.

Usually, though, it starts with one small act, be it rejection or rebellion. Each subsequent one not dealt with by Holy Spirit, through forgiveness or repentance or both, leads a person farther away from his or her destiny. Two individuals, one from the past and one from the present, highlight the freedom of choice.

Remember Pete, from Chapter Two? Pete's history will seem familiar to some. Throughout his formative years and into high school, he went to church with his family. Once his college career started, he lived his own life, did his own thing. Attendance at the house of worship? Spotty, at best. Belief in the Bible? Nominal. Throughout his childhood, he didn't believe he measured up to his father's approval; hence, the father-son relationship lacked a solid foundation.

These attitudes carried over in his marriage to Michelle.* Shortly after their wedding vows, his wife committed her life to the Lord. She loved God and desired a deep, intimate walk with Him. She prayed diligently for Pete and asked others to join her. Breakthroughs, small and big, came at regular intervals. Eventually, he also accepted Jesus in his heart.

Unfortunately, Pete did not close the two open doors to the perverse spirit once he came to the Lord. He refused to walk through the necessary steps of forgiveness regarding his father's rejection, and he refused to repent of his rebellion. Aware of these issues, Michelle continued her intercession on his behalf.

One day, she came home from work and discovered a new three-pound can of coffee missing. She didn't drink any, but Pete did, and at the time, coffee was expensive. Soon he walked through the door, his face aglow. Before she could ask about the absent can, Pete burst out with his story. During his morning prayer time, God had told him to quit drinking coffee, so he donated it to a local charity. The couple laughed and rejoiced together. The Lord was definitely moving in them individually and in their marriage.

About six weeks later, their destinies reached a crossroads. The church they attended brought in a guest speaker for special meetings. Michelle knew the two of them needed to go together. She did all she could to persuade Pete to join her, but he adamantly refused. He chose to make a trip to see his family. It was the wrong choice.

The morning after Pete arrived home, Michelle noticed a coffee cup in his hand. She questioned him. His response? "A little coffee never hurt anyone."

Without getting the exact details, Michelle knew Pete had turned away from the Word of the Lord. He chose rebellion over obedience. Slowly at first, then picking up speed like an out-of-control bicycle careening down a hill, his walk with the Lord skewed more and more. Their marriage went from full of hope to full of despair. They eventually separated and later divorced.

At one time, Pete knew the Lord called him into the ministry. Deliberate choices led him from the will of God. Today only a shell remains of the man God destined him to be. Since the gifts and callings are without repentance, Pete may yet fulfill his destiny (Romans 11:29). However, at this point, he still walks a twisted and tortuous path that began with a cup of coffee.

Let's turn our attention to a man from the past, Noah Webster. Though I already dedicated a chapter to him, I did a little research about Mr. Webster and found him to be a very interesting subject. While Noah grew up in a Christian home, he was not always the devout believer we've come to know. His own doubts as a young man and influences from the wrong college crowd led him on a bit of a crooked path. His famous *The American Spelling Book*, more commonly referred to as the *Blue-Backed Speller*, was completely secular, albeit very patriotic.[82] No names of God. No Bible verses. No mention of writings from powerful preachers of his day. He went so far as to write, "Let sacred things be appropriated for sacred purposes." [83]

Not until 1808, at the age of fifty, did Webster undergo a profound religious experience as revival broke out in the fledgling country. A now devout Christian, he began extolling the importance of Christian influence on government leaders. While he started his famous dictionary *An American Dictionary of the English Language* in 1801, seven years prior to his conversion, the following quote found in the preface portrays his radical change:

"In my view, the Christian religion is the most important and one of the first things in which all children, under a free government ought to be instructed . . . No truth is more evident to my mind than that the Christian religion must be the basis of any government intended to secure the rights and privileges of a free people". [84]

Think for a minute about God's blueprints for this man. Before the Lord knit him together in his mother's womb, He purposed that Noah would write the first American dictionary. The divine plan of heaven. Look at other quotes revealing his transformation:

"All the miseries and evils which men suffer from vice, crime, ambition, injustice, oppression, slavery and war, proceed from their despising or neglecting the precepts contained in the Bible." [85]

"When you become entitled to exercise the right of voting for public officers, let it be impressed on your mind that God commands you to choose for rulers, 'just men who will rule in the fear of God.'" [86]

"Almost all the civil liberty now enjoyed in the world owes its origin to the principles of the [C]hristian religion." [87]

A man of God establishing a work so profound, the effects continue for generations.

Noah turned back to God, God gave him honor among men, and he fulfilled his destiny. Pete turned away from God, is despised among men, and his God-given destiny hangs in the balance. Noah and Pete. Both made choices. Both choices brought forth fruit. However, one tastes sweet; the other leaves a bitter taste in the mouth.

Destinies. We all have one. Skewed or straight, we each walk a path. Even though the perverse spirit actively tempts and seduces us to follow his crooked trail, the ultimate choice rests with us. Regardless of what we choose, God does not despair. He doesn't plumb the depths of desolation. Instead, the very essence of His being exudes hope. Why? Because He designed a future for each of us, and He knows the end from the beginning. He wins! And because He wins, we win!

To help us ensure our victory, God sent Holy Spirit to live on the inside of us. And get this—Holy Spirit loves what He does! He looks forward every day to helping us fulfill our destinies. He delights with the prospect of getting us to the next step in our journey, all culminating in our transformation. Why? So we can have the same image as Jesus (2 Corinthians 3:18). Who wouldn't love a job like that? Making sure a child of God looks just like his Father!

If you're examining your walk with God and only see a crooked road, don't lose heart. It wasn't too late for Noah Webster. It isn't too late for you. God will make the crooked places straight. He promised.

CHAPTER 8

A New Beginning

Is this really the end? No more crooked places? Everything made straight? Are you sure? Can I truly shine like a star?

Finally. Is it possible? Am I really at the end? It appears so. Nine months longer than I thought it would take. Prophetic? Maybe. Nine months of carrying this "baby" brought out buried emotions and long-forgotten memories. I dealt with raw pain, fear I didn't want to face, anger I didn't want to let go of, and rejection still fresh in my mind. Weeks went by without a single word written down. Many days I wanted to quit. Some moments I despaired of living.

But God was relentless in bringing forth the finished work, not only with this book, but also in me. That's not to say I've arrived. I think Paul said it best in his letter to the Philippians:

Not that I have already attained, or am already perfected; but I press on, that I may lay hold of that for which Christ Jesus has also laid hold of me. Brethren, I do not count myself to have apprehended; but one thing I do, forgetting those things which are behind and reaching forward to those things which are ahead, I press toward the goal for the prize of the upward call of God in Christ Jesus. (3:12–14)

I like the way the King James Version puts verse 14, "I press toward the mark for the prize of the high calling of God in Christ Jesus." The original meaning for *sin* means *to miss the mark* and *to not share in the prize*.[88] I don't want to miss the mark anymore, but I definitely want to share in the prize. I know you feel the same way. Come with me as we lift our voices before the throne of God:

Father God, we purpose in our hearts to press toward that mark. We want the prize of the high calling you have for us. We want what Jesus, our Savior, holds in His hands for us—the destiny Father, Son, and Holy Spirit planned with us in mind before the foundation of the world.

Lord, we want the crooked places made straight in our lives. We're ready to walk straight paths leading to the Highway of Holiness. We want fresh starts and new beginnings. We want our lives to be shining examples to lead others out of darkness. But we can't do it on our own. We can only rest in your promises, the Yes and Amen ones found in Christ Jesus. Glory, hallelujah to our Great God, Everlasting Father, Prince of Peace.

Before we close the book, let's look at those promises one last time:

Every valley shall be exalted and every mountain and hill brought low; The *crooked* places shall be made straight and the rough places smooth. (Isa. 40:4)

I will bring the blind by a way they did not know; I will lead them in paths they have not known.

I will make darkness light before them, and *crooked* places straight.
These things I will do for them, and not forsake them. (Isa. 42:16)

I will go before you and make the *crooked* places straight;
I will break in pieces the gates of bronze and cut the bars of iron.
I will give you the treasures of darkness and hidden riches of secret places,
That you may know that I, the LORD, who call you by your name,
Am the God of Israel. (Isa. 45:2–3)

Do not remember the former things, nor consider the things of old.
Behold, I will do a new thing, now it shall spring forth;
Shall you not know it?
I will even make a road in the wilderness . . .
This people I have formed for Myself; they shall declare My praise.
(Isa. 43:18–19a, 21)

This God, *our God*, deserves nothing less than all we have, all we are, and all
we hope to be:

Only You, God,
lift us from the depths of despair into your marvelous grace.
Only You, Lord,
bring down every mountain of pride in our lives so we bow
down in humble adoration before our holy King.
Only You, Captain of the Host,
remove every stumbling block and make a way of escape
as we praise your name.
Only You, Sun of Righteousness,
open our blind eyes so we can behold your glory.
Only You, Shepherd of our souls,
lead us in paths of righteousness for your name's sake.
Only You, Father of Lights,
bring us out of darkness into your marvelous light.

Only You, Faithful and True Witness,
never leave us nor abandon us.
Only You, Man of War,
deliver us from our captivity into the glorious
liberty of Jesus Christ.
Only You, Light of the Morning,
see treasure in our darkness and hidden riches in the
secret places of our hearts.
Only You, Abba Father,
speak forth our names with destiny in the sound.
Only You, Alpha and Omega,
give us a new beginning with a glorious finish.
Only You, Jehovah God,
make the crooked places straight and lead us on the
Highway of Holiness.

Although the pages of this book may come to an end, our praises of you, Eternal God, Lamb upon the Throne, Spirit of the Living God, are only beginning. As long as we have breath, they will ring out in the earth, and then for all eternity, as we behold you, face-to-face, and join the twenty-four elders and the angels around your throne in worship:

Amen! Blessing and glory and wisdom,
thanksgiving and honor and power and might,
be to our God forever and ever. Amen. (Rev. 7:12)

We give You thanks, O Lord God Almighty,
the One who is and who was and who is to come,
because You have taken Your great power and reigned. (Rev. 11:17)

Lord God Almighty, let your scepter rule in the midst of our enemies as we stake our claim in the inheritance you have given us: Crooked places made straight. Shining stars in the darkest of nights.

Hallelujah to the Lamb!

A CALL TO ARMS

Arms? My left and right ones handle things just fine. Oh, wait a minute. You're not talking about limbs; you're talking about going into battle. Now that I finished reading your book, I feel like taking on Genghis Khan. Well, not really, but I am definitely more prepared and better equipped. Still, I don't want to lose ground. What's my next step?

I am thrilled to hear you say that. And you're right; you don't want to lose ground. Below you will find suggestions to help you not only hold your ground, but take back what the enemy has stolen:

- Continue praying for yourself and others. By the way, the prayers I wrote are starting points. Holy Spirit may give you something completely different to pray in your situation.
- Share the book with others, including your pastor.
- Share the book on your social media sites.
- Form a prayer group to deal with the perverse spirit in your personal lives, families, churches, cities, etc.
- Form a Christian Reading Club and read this together.
- Go to my website. You'll find additional tools and great resources, including a free Bible study and a free prayer booklet with all of the prayers from *Making Crooked Places Straight*: www.PS2710.com

On a personal note, I want to say how proud I am of you for pressing through to victory. You may not feel victorious. Life may not look victorious. But through His cross, Jesus made you victorious!

Hooray! Hallelujah! Amen!

ABOUT THE AUTHOR

A passionate lover of Jesus for over 30 years, Penelope Kaye makes her home in Billings, Montana's largest city. With a strong Pentecostal/charismatic background, her love for word studies and passion for setting captives free led her to write and teach numerous Bible studies, including "Adorning the Bride" and "Pools of Anointing in Worship." She shares at prayer retreats, women's conferences, and the pulpit of her local church, First Baptist Church. Penelope's heart for children led her to teach them in a variety of venues as well as author several soon-to-be published children's picture books. Newly ordained in ministry, she has written newspaper columns on prayer, faith, and the Bible for area newspapers and is an annual book reviewer for the High Plains BookFest. Her devotional, "In the Dark and Loving It" won "Best Devotional" for the Oregon Writers Cascade Awards. When she's not writing, teaching, and speaking, you can find her in the Big Sky Country eating blueberries anytime of the day.

ACKNOWLEDGMENTS

For years I read this page in other books, looking at the names of people who were instrumental in turning someone's idea into reality. Now it's my turn, and I find myself overwhelmed with gratitude to those who made it possible. Please know the list isn't inclusive. Many of you impacted my life in countless ways. If I named every person who prayed for me, encouraged me, battled for me, and loved me, not just through this journey, but to help bring me to the woman I am today, I would fill another book. I love and appreciate you more than you can know.

Holly Joy and Rebekah, my favorite first- and second-born. Too little space and too many words to describe my love for you.

Teresa and Brenda. I wouldn't have survived the word study without your prayers.

My intercessors who prayed for me while writing the manuscript. You carried me when I didn't think I could stand, and you did not stop until I finished.

My intercessors who prayed for me during the publishing process. Your prayers made this experience feel as though I walked on air through the months of watching the impossible unfold.

Karen. You are for me always and forever a hundred, thousand, million times. I couldn't ask for anything more.

Heidi. You let me yell and scream and sob my guts out during the writing of the manuscript those many years ago. Your worth is far beyond anything this world offers. I am honored and humbled by your extravagant gifts to the Lord and His bride.

Linaya and Wanda, my editors. Without your expertise and guidance, this would be third-rate instead of first-class! Endless thanks to you.

Treasure State Scribes. Your joy and enthusiasm for writing and trust in me as your leader delights my heart.

Morgan James Publishing. You are a truly first-class publishing house. Special thanks to Terry Whalin for not giving up on me, Wes Taylor who trusted me with this work even though I didn't trust him, and David Hancock who believed in me when I didn't quite believe in myself. Without the support of these three men, *Making Crooked Places Straight* would still be in the closet.

My Abba Father, my Beloved Bridegroom, my Best Friend. This book exists only because of your relentless faithfulness, your love beyond the deepest oceans, your unfathomable forgiveness, and your indescribable joy. You are the reason for my life on earth. I love and worship you beyond words.

SPECIAL THANKS

Without the support of the following people, *Making Crooked Places Straight* would still be in the closet. I am humbled and honored that you believed in me and were willing to share in this wild, crazy adventure. While "thank you" doesn't seem enough on paper, I have no doubt that great will be your heavenly rewards. God bless each of you.

Albert & Wilma LaRance
Arnetta Hodgman
Barbara Bueno
Biff & Brenda Hagstrom
Bonnie Scherer
Connie Karst
Dennis Petermann
Eleanor Halsey
Heidi Hoffner
Jan Feil
Judy Kastrop
Karen Christian
Kelly
Laura Esquibel
Linaya Leaf
Lisha Denney/Country Pearl Crush
Lori Bonifay

Lorie Pelatt
Lupe Brown
Marion Albrecht
Mary Jo Mueller
Melody Wethermon
Natalie Marshall
Pam Stusek
Pat & David Thibault
Ray & MaryAnn Kunkel
Robin Grinsteiner
Ron Stevens
Ross Lieuallen
Vickie Swander
Anonymous S1
Anonymous S2

An American Dictionary of the English Language

As I researched Noah Webster, I came across his 1828 edition of *An American Dictionary of the English Language* and looked at his original definitions. I am including meanings from this edition for various forms of *perverse, crooked, froward, iniquity, untoward*:

Perverse:

1. Literally, turned aside; hence, distorted from the right.
2. Obstinate in the wrong; disposed to be contrary; stubborn; untractable.
3. Cross; petulant; peevish; disposed to cross and vex.

Pervert:

1. To turn from truth, propriety, or from its proper purpose; to distort from its true use or end; as, to pervert reason by misdirecting it; to pervert the laws by misinterpreting and misapplying them; to pervert

justice; to pervert the meaning of an author; to pervert nature; to pervert truth.

2. To turn from the right; to corrupt.

He in the serpent had perverted Eve.

[Pervert, when used of persons, usually implies evil design.]

Crooked:

1. Bent; curved; curving; winding.
2. Winding in moral conduct; devious; froward; perverse; going out of the path of rectitude; given to obliquity or wandering from duty.

Crookedness:

1. A winding, bending or turning; curvity; curvature; inflection.
2. Perverseness; untowardness; deviation from rectitude; iniquity; obliquity of conduct.

Froward:

1. Perverse, that is, turning from, with aversion or reluctance; not willing to yield or comply with what is required; unyielding; ungovernable; refractory; disobedient; peevish; as a froward child.

Iniquity:

1. Injustice; unrighteousness; a deviation from rectitude; as the iniquity of war; the iniquity of the slave trade.
2. Want of rectitude in principle; as a malicious prosecution originating in the iniquity of the author.
3. A particular deviation from rectitude; a sin or crime; wickedness; any act of injustice.
4. Original want of holiness or depravity.

Untoward:

1. Froward; perverse; refractory; not easily guided or taught.
2. Awkward; ungraceful; as untoward words.

3. Inconvenient; troublesome; unmanageable; as an untoward vow.

Untowardly:
1. In a froward or perverse manner; perversely; ungainly.
2. Awkward; perverse; froward.

(Note: For those interested in looking up other original definitions, you will find the link listed in the references.)

SCRIPTURE REFERENCES

The following is a list of all the Scriptures quoted and referenced:

Genesis
1:1–10
1:26
2:7
2:8
2:15
2:16–17
3:1b–5
3:17–19
8:21
11:6b
15
15:18
17:1
22:14

Exodus
12:23
23:8

Leviticus
25:23–34
26:40, 41b–42a
27:17–25

Numbers
23:19

Deuteronomy
8:17
8:18
32:30

Joshua
6
6:20

Judges

2 Chronicles
7:14

Job
5:13
33:15–28
34:11–12
41

Psalms
2:4
17:8
18
27:13–14
31:9–11
31:15
32:1–2
32:5–6a
34:10b
35:27
36:3
37:34a
38:18–19a
38:21–22

40:12b

49:5

49:6–8a

51:1–3, 12–13

51:6

52:1, 5, 7

62:10b

64:2b–3

78:38–39

79:8

85:2

90:17

91:11–12

94:18

94:20

101:1–4

103:1, 3, 10

103:4

107:17–20

112:1, 3

119:11

119:40

119:133

125:3–5a

125:5

130:7–8

133

149:5–9

Proverbs

2:10–15

2:12b–15

2:12–15

4:24

6:2

6:12

6:14

10:2

10:9

10:16a

10:19

10:22

10:31, 32

11:3b

11:28a

12:8

13:12

14:1

14:2b

14:14

15:4

16:6

16:28

16:29–30

17:20

18:21

19:1

19:3

19:28

21:8

22:4

22:8

23:5

23:31–33

28:6

28:18

31:4b, 5

Ecclesiastes

3:9, 11a, 12–13

4:12

5:19–20

Isaiah

1:19

5:20, 24

7:14–15

10:27

14

14:13–14

19:1–4a, 5, 8a

19:9b–10, 13–14

27:1

28:1

33:6

33:20

33:24

35

40:2

40:4

40:31

42:16

43:1

43:18–19a, 21

45:2–3

49:16

52:12

53:3

53:5–6, 11–12

54:17
57:17
59:6–8

Jeremiah
8:5
22:29
23:36
29:11
31:34b
33:8

Ezekiel
28:12b–15, 17
36:33

Daniel
2:20–21
4:27a

Hosea
14:4

Joel
2

Micah
7:18–19

Zechariah
4:7

Malachi
2:6
4:1, 2a, 3a

Matthew
1:18–19
8:16
9:32–33
12:37
16:23
18:7
18:20
19
23:27–28
24:12
26:14–15a
26:56b
26:74
28:19–20

Mark
1:39
3:21
4
4:5–6, 16–17
5:1–15
7:25–30
9:14–27
15:34

Luke
4:28–29a
10:19

John
6:60–61, 66
8:32
9:3
12:32
14:6, 16–17a

Acts
2:40
3:26
4:8–12
4:31
12
13
17:6
19
20:28–30

Romans
1
4:7
5:8
8:14–17a
8:21–22
8:26
8:37
11:29
16:20

1 Corinthians
10:11
13:8

2 Corinthians
3:18
7:10–11
9:8–9
10:4
12:9

Galatians
4:6–7
4:22–31
6:2

Ephesians
1:6
2:8–9
5
6
6:12
6:15

Philippians
1:7
1:10
2:10–11
2:12–16a
3:12–14
4:13

Colossians
3:3

1 Timothy
2:1–2

4:1–2
6:5

2 Timothy
2:19
3:1–4
4:2

Titus
2:13–14

Hebrews
1:3
2:14, 17a
4:12
8:12
10:17
10:24–25
11:3
12:2

James
3:6, 8
5:14, 16

1 Peter
2:18
4:17

1 John
1 John
3:8

2 John
8

Revelation
1:6
3:17
7:12
11:17

REFERENCES

Eagle Ministries International. "Sweet Victory." *Eagle Song III*. EMI, 1990.

Ellis, Joseph J. *After the Revolution: Profiles of Early American Culture*. New York, NY: W.W. Norton, 1979.

Snyder, Alan K. *Defining Noah Webster: Mind and Morals in the Early Republic*. Lanham, MD: University Press of America, 1990.

Stone, Nathan. *Names of God*. Chicago, IL: The Moody Bible Institute of Chicago, 1944.

Strong, James. *The New Strong's Exhaustive Concordance of the Bible*. Nashville, TN: Thomas Nelson Publishers, 1990.

Webster, Noah. *An American Dictionary of the English Language*. New York, NY: S. Converse, 1828.

Webster, Noah. *History of the United States*. New Haven, CT: Durrie & Peck, 1832.

Wright, Henry W. *A More Excellent Way*. New Kensington, PA: Whitaker House, 1999, 2005, 2009.

http://www.academia.edu/8417718/The_legend_of_Annu-Nagi_
Mythology_and_History_of_Naga_People_and_Queen_Gaidinliu_of_
Naga, accessed February 18, 2018.

https://brandongaille.com/44-teenage-runaway-statistics/, accessed February
18, 2018.

https://www.healthline.com/health-news/the-debate-over-terminating-
down-syndrome-pregnancies#1, accessed March 17, 2018.

https://www.justice.gov/archives/dag/page/file/914031/download, accessed
February 18, 2018.

https://my.kcm.org/p-43-covenant-made-by-blood-cd-series.aspx, accessed
February 18, 2018.

https://www.nationaleatingdisorders.org/learn/general-information/what-
are-eating-disorders, accessed February 17, 2018.

https://ovc.ncjrs.gov/ncvrw2016/content/section-6/PDF/2016NCVRW_6_
FinancialCrime-508.pdf, accessed February 18, 2018.

http://www.pastoralcareinc.com/statistics/clarification-on-statistics/,
accessed February 17, 2018.

http://webstersdictionary1828.com/

http://www.wf-lawyers.com/divorce-statistics-and-facts/, accessed March
17, 2018.

https://en.wikipedia.org/w/index.php?title=List_of_
coups_d%27%C3%A9tat_and_coup_attempts&oldid=8298445, accessed
March 17, 2018.

https://en.wikipedia.org/w/index.php?title=Special:CiteThisPage&page=There_Was_a_Crooked_Man&id=, accessed March 17, 2018.

ENDNOTES

Chapter One

1   James Strong, *The New Strong's Exhaustive Concordance of the Bible* (Nashville, TN: Thomas Nelson Publishers, 1990).

2   The chicken scratch page contained phrases, thoughts, and revelations I jotted down after finishing the initial work. I didn't do an in-depth study with any of it, mainly because I was sick of looking at it.

3   Ibid., ref. no. *714.*

Chapter Two

4   James Strong, *The New Strong's Exhaustive Concordance of the Bible* (Nashville, TN: Thomas Nelson Publishers, 1990), ref. no. 3399.

5   Ibid., ref. no. 5999.

6   Ibid., ref. no. *3859.*

7   Ibid., ref. no. 5557.

8   Ibid.

9   https://en.wikipedia.org/w/index.php?title=List_of_coups_d%27%C3%A9tat_and_coup_attempts&oldid=829844555.

10 Strong, *The New Strong's Exhaustive Concordance*, ref. no. 5791.

11 Ibid., ref. no. 2019; 3868; 6141; 8419.

12 Ibid., ref. no. *4646.*

13 Ibid., ref. no. 5771, 5753.

14 Ibid., ref. no. *4646.*

15 Ibid., ref. no. 2015.

16 Ibid., ref. no. 5558.

17 Ibid., ref. no. 7667.

18 Ibid., ref. no. 4297; 5186; 6140; 6141; *1294*.

19 Ibid., ref. no. 5186.

20 Ibid., ref. no. 6141.

21 Nathan Stone, *Names of God* (Chicago, IL: The Moody Bible Institute of Chicago, 1944), p. 35.

22 Strong, *The New Strong's Exhaustive Concordance*, ref. no. 3070.

23 https://www.nationaleatingdisorders.org/learn/general-information/what-are-eating-disorders, accessed February 17, 2018.

24 Strong, *The New Strong's Exhaustive Concordance*, ref. no. 6140.

25 Ibid., ref. no. 4297

26 Ibid., ref. no. *4762*.

27 Ibid., ref. no. 1921.

28 Ibid., ref. no. 7999.

29 Ibid., ref. no. 5999.

30 Ibid., ref. no 5998.

31 Ibid., ref. no. *3859*.

32 Ibid., ref. no *5147*.

33 Ibid., ref. no. 5999.

34 http://www.pastoralcareinc.com/statistics/clarification-on-statistics/, accessed March 17, 2018.

35 Strong, *The New Strong's Exhaustive Concordance*, ref. no. *3859*.

36 Ibid., ref. no. 1942.

37 Ibid., ref. no. 3399.

38 Regarding His reference to thyme and stew: I have a delicious recipe for vegetable stew. The key ingredient is fresh thyme. The Lord made a play on words about the importance of time in His plans.

39 Ibid., ref. no. 7726; 7725.

40 Ibid., ref. no. *654*.

41 Ibid., ref. no. *575*.

42 Ibid., ref. no. *4762*.

43 https://en.wikipedia.org/w/index.php?title=Special:CiteThisPage&page=There_Was_a_Crooked_Man&id=827232166, accessed March 17, 2018.

44 Strong, *The New Strong's Exhaustive Concordance*, ref. no. 6117.

45 Ibid., ref. no. 1281.

46 Ibid., ref. no. 1272.

47 Ibid., ref. no. 8419.

48 Ibid., ref. no. 5753.

49 https://ovc.ncjrs.gov/ncvrw2016/content/section-6/PDF/2016NCVRW_6_FinancialCrime-508.pdf, accessed February 18, 2018.

50 https://brandongaille.com/44-teenage-runaway-statistics/ ,accessed February 18, 2018.

51 https://www.justice.gov/archives/dag/page/file/914031/download, accessed February 18, 2018.

52 https://en.wikipedia.org/w/index.php?title=Incarceration_in_the_United_States&oldid=828591659.

53 Strong, *The New Strong's Exhaustive Concordance*, ref. no. 8138.

Chapter Three

54 James Strong, *The New Strong's Exhaustive Concordance of the Bible* (Nashville, TN: Thomas Nelson Publishers, 1990), ref. no. 5766.

55 Ibid., ref. no. *5485*.

Chapter Four

56 http://www.wf-lawyers.com/divorce-statistics-and-facts/, accessed March 17, 2018.

57 James Strong, *The New Strong's Exhaustive Concordance of the Bible* (Nashville, TN: Thomas Nelson Publishers, 1990), ref. no. 7667.

58 Ibid., ref. no. 8582.

59 Ibid., ref. no. *1294*.

60 Ibid., ref. no. *4762*.

Chapter Five

61 http://www.academia.edu/8417718/The_legend_of_AnnuNagi_Mythology_and_History_of_Naga_People_and_Queen_Gaidinliu_of_Naga, accessed February 18, 2018.

62 James Strong, *The New Strong's Exhaustive Concordance of the Bible* (Nash-

ville, TN: Thomas Nelson Publishers, 1990), ref. no. 4297.

63 Henry W. Wright, *A More Excellent Way* (New Kensington, PA: Whitaker House, 1999, 2005, 2009).

64 Strong, *The New Strong's Exhaustive Concordance*, ref. no. *4646*.

65 Ibid., ref. no. 8378.

66 Salvation includes deliverance, health, prosperity, and victory.

67 https://www.healthline.com/health-news/the-debate-over-terminating-down-syndrome-pregnancies#1, accessed March 17, 2018.

Chapter Six

68 James Strong, *The New Strong's Exhaustive Concordance of the Bible* (Nashville, TN: Thomas Nelson Publishers, 1990), ref. no. *1411*.

69 Ibid., ref. no. *1743, 1412, 1411*.

70 Ibid., ref. no. *1415, 1411*.

71 Ibid., ref. no. 7999.

72 Ibid., ref. no. 2421.

73 Ibid., ref. no. 2617.

74 Ibid., ref. no. *25*.

75 https://my.kcm.org/p-43-covenant-made-by-blood-cd-series.aspx.

76 Strong, *The New Strong's Exhaustive Concordance*, ref. no. 3533.

77 Ibid., ref. no. 7564; 7562.

78 Ibid., ref. no. *4624*.

79 Ibid., ref. no. 6588.

80 Ibid., ref. no. *2480, 2479*.

81 Eagle Ministries International, "Sweet Victory," *Eagle Song III*, (EMI, 1990). Used with permission.

Chapter Seven

82 Noah Webster, *The American Spelling Book* (Philadelphia, PA: Johnson & Warner, 1809).

83 Contributors: Joseph J. Ellis – author, *After the Revolution: Profiles of Early American Culture* (New York: W. W. Norton, 1979), 175.

84 Noah Webster, *An American Dictionary of the English Language* (New York:

S. Converse, 1828), preface.

85 Noah Webster, *History of the United States* (New Haven: Durrie & Peck, 1832), 339.

86 Ibid., 336.

87 Ibid., 300.

Chapter Eight

88 James Strong, *The New Strong's Exhaustive Concordance of the Bible* (Nashville, TN: Thomas Nelson Publishers, 1990), ref. no. *264*.